HOW TO SAY
HARD
THINGS
THE
Easy Way

HOW TO SAY
HARD THINGS
THE
Easy Way

Richard Walters

WORD PUBLISHING
Dallas·London·Vancouver·Melbourne

HOW TO SAY HARD THINGS THE EASY WAY

All Scripture quotations are from the New International Version, copy-
right © 1983 International Bible Society, used by permission of
Zondervan Bible Publishers.

Some chapters of this book quote, or are adapted from, other publica-
tions copyrighted by Richard P. Walters, and are used by permission:
Amity: Friendship in Action, 4th ed., 1982; *Boldness: The Proactive
Lifestyle*, 1982; *Practicing the Skills of Boldness*, 1982; *Anger Storms*,
1985; *Tell It Like It Is: Skills in Confrontational Feedback*, 1985; *Bridges:
The Caring Connection in Disaster Response*, 1990; *Life Builder Training*, 1991. Information about these materials may be obtained by ad-
dressing the author in care of Word Publishing, 5221 N. O'Connor
Boulevard, Irving, Texas 75039.

Library of Congress Cataloging-in-Publication Data

Walters, Richard P., 1935–
     How to say hard things the easy way / Richard Walters.
       p. cm.
     ISBN 0–8499–3272–6
     1. Conduct of life. 2. Oral communication.
   BJ1581.2.W34   1991
   158'.2–dc20   91–20330
                                                                  CIP

123459 AGF 654321

Printed in the United States of America

CONTENTS

PART ONE

You Can Master the Skills of the Easy Way

1

You Can Move Past Obstacles and Reach Your Goals

Mary laughs about it now. "But at the time," she says, "I was less fun to be around than a flu epidemic. I was a violin string about to snap. My husband said I was as cuddly as a brick. It all scared me plenty, but the fear just got me more up tight."

Mary wouldn't say *no* when she needed to. So demands on her time and energy piled up.

And she wouldn't *ask* when she needed to. She didn't look out for herself. So gloom and frustration piled up, too.

Things broke the day her six-year-old, Jo-Jo, put the gerbil in the aquarium for swimming lessons. When Mary heard the splashing and giggling, she dashed into the den, saw the situation—and exploded. She shouted, shaking her finger at Jo-Jo, who grabbed the gerbil and fled to the bathroom.

Mary sat on the couch, shaking with a surge of fear, anger, and despair, while in her mind she was furiously shouting condemnation at herself. She wanted to apologize to Jo-Jo. She also wanted to talk candidly to her husband about her feelings. She wanted to quit being a pushover—a *coward,* she called herself—in every hard situation. She wanted to move past the obstacles on her road of life, but she didn't know how.

Jo-Jo and Geri the Gerbil recuperated faster than Mary, who sat forlornly in the den, mentally replaying a series of old events as though watching a video tape. *Lowlights of a Low Life,* she privately called these memories.

She remembered the time she had thrown away a brand-new pair of pantyhose. They were defective—if you consider both legs stitched together all the way to the ankles a defect—but she had been unwilling to go back and ask for a refund. Instead, she threw them out.

Mary remembered the time a neighbor had gossiped about the family and how she had not been willing to confront the neighbor about what she had said. With anger at herself for being so passive, Mary had blushed whenever she looked out the window and saw the neighbor.

And she recalled the year during high school when she was a part-time waitress at Tweeties and had worked there longer than anyone before she got a raise. She felt again the sting of the boss's off-hand remark: "Why didn't you ask sooner?"

Her library of regrets seemed endless. Each short sketch brought again the pain she'd felt when the situation had first happened.

At length she roused herself wearily and went into the kitchen. In slow motion she baked a pumpkin pie—a token of peace, a gesture of apology, a purchase of friendship.

Pie in the oven, she sat at the kitchen table, heavy with gloom. The timer went off at last. The air was cozy with the sweet tang of pumpkin as she lifted out the pie.

The phone rang. She set the pie on the chair in front of her and answered the phone on the wall behind her.

It was Lyddie—the friend of the never-ending phone call. Once, after listening patiently through a call of interminable length from Lyddie, Mary had said to her husband, "I could have read the *Encyclopedia Britannica* while I was listening to her." He replied, "You could have *written* it."

As Lyddie prattled on—about what, Mary couldn't have told you—Mary stood waiting with smoldering impatience. She was angry at Lyddie for her endless talk—and at herself for being unwilling to interrupt and end the one-sided conversation. She shifted from right foot to left and again to right. Then, with relief, she heard Lyddie say, "It was nice hearing from you," and hang up.

Mary had just hung up when the phone rang again. It was Mrs. Dorry from the grade school. Would Mary help chaperone a field trip next Tuesday? Of course she would, Mary replied from habit, as anger again boiled within her. *Why didn't I say no?* she asked herself.

With shaking hand, she put the phone back on the hook. She turned and stood with hands flat on the kitchen table, shaking her head from side to side and muttering, "Every day I get busier. Every day I try harder. Every day I get farther behind."

In her despair she sighed, "It's no use to try," and slumped onto the chair. Onto the pie—the warm, smooshy pumpkin pie.

Mary's trip down the road of life was littered with obstacles that complicated her journey, kept her from enjoying herself, and prevented her from reaching her goals. She didn't know how to say *no* or how to confront those who had treated her unjustly. She couldn't bring herself to apologize for her own wrongdoings. Long-winded friends often trapped her with drawn-out tales of gossip and trashy talk. With growing frustration and anger, Mary endured these obstacles because she didn't know how to say the hard things that needed to be said.

Like Mary, you have goals, too. *Great!*

You, too, are swiftly moving down the road of life. *Greater still!*

Suddenly, though, you trip over the same rocks that blocked Mary's journey—obstacles between you and your goals. *Not so great, but normal.*

An obstacle may even look as big as a mountain—a humongous problem between you and where you want to go. *That's normal, too, but lousy.*

It may be so frustrating you want to quit trying. Like Mary, you might like to sit down and cry. But you *can* get where you want to go. *This book will help you get past the mountains of obstacles and reach your goals.* It will teach you how to say hard things the easy way.

Usually an obstacle has a face on it. It's the result of something another person has done to or thought about you—or hasn't done or thought. When you see a face on the mountain and it isn't Mount Rushmore, what do you do?

This book will guide you. It will give you specific tactics to use to overcome the obstacles you meet. And it includes straight talk about the source of power that enables you to do what you *know* you need to do.

The Face on Mount Obstacle

People problems are rarely fixed without talking to the person involved. "That's easy for you to say," you might want to tell me right now. "But it's not so easy to do. You don't know the obstacle people in my life." No, I don't. But I know how people get past mountains to reach their goals. This book will tell you how to have those talks you need to have, to say the hard things you need to say—the easy way.

The obstacle could hold you back in life, but *it doesn't have to.* That's up to you.

Why You Win Every Time

Success is guaranteed. Well . . . like most guarantees, it is only *partly* guaranteed. There are two types of success you can have in people problems: (1) the other person cooperates with you, and (2) *you* cooperate with you. Often, you can get both of these, but you can *always* have the latter. You can *always* have the satisfaction of knowing that you did your best to help yourself.

No matter how appealingly you present yourself, no matter how much sense you make, another person can reject you and keep you from getting what you want and deserve. The other person may not cooperate. You may give good and receive evil. We can never change that.

But when you go to the mountain and start to climb it, tunnel into it, or go around it, you cooperate with yourself. That is always rewarding. When you do what you can to help yourself, being forceful and respectful with the other person, you *will* feel better.

You grow when you deal wisely with obstacles. Whether you win or lose, you win. Taking the trip to go around (or over or through) the obstacle *always* brings you to a better place. You'll be stronger, wiser, and more at ease with yourself and the world, no matter what.

What You Need to Move Ahead

To travel past obstacle mountains you need a plan, techniques, and power. Then you put them together with wisdom.

The plan is like a map, a guide to help you get to a goal. Techniques are like cars to travel in. This book offers you a map (plan) and a fleet of cars (techniques). It will give you basic, down-to-earth preparation in plain language. Then the book will help you select a car and drive it. Along the way, I'll point out the shortcuts and help you avoid wrong turns.

But a good plan and techniques are not enough. You need a strong engine to move the car. The engine provides the power to do what you know how to do. But you also need a steering system so you can take the curves in the road as you follow the map. This steering system is wisdom.

And you must decide you want to make the trip. Many of us have been a little timid about getting out on the road, even to travel to those good places we'd like to enjoy. Maybe that's true for you. If it is, you will especially benefit from chapter 5, which points you to the source of power and wisdom, and describes how to access the power to get "out of the garage" and onto the road so you can go where the rewards are.

As you travel toward your goals it will be helpful to have a friend travel with you. The two of you can talk through the examples, try out problem-solving ideas on each other, rehearse conversations, and encourage one another. You probably know several people who could benefit from this book as much as you. Pick one, then do yourselves a favor; work on this together. It's more fun, and you'll learn faster. But you can do it alone if you prefer.

How to Get Help Quickly from This Book

This book describes many techniques. Three are especially valuable because they are forceful in many situations. These are listening (chapter 2), "I-statements" (chapter 3), and confrontation (chapter 4). You should read those chapters next, plus chapters 5 (accessing the power) and 6 (putting it all together). I also urge you to continue your reading through chapter 7 (how to say no). You're certain to run into situations in which those skills will be useful. Also, chapter 7 will help you catch on to the teaching pattern followed in most of the other chapters, and that will save you some time.

After you've read the first seven chapters, go directly to the chapter that deals with your biggest obstacle. For most topics, all the information is contained within its own chapter. When additional information is needed, I'll direct you to parts of other chapters you should read.

Grab the map, start the car, and get ready to go past—wa-a-a-y past—your obstacles. Let's roll!

2

You Can Talk with People about Their Needs

While I was writing this book I mentioned the title and some of the topics to a friend, who replied, "You've got to be kidding! There *can't* be an easy way to do *those* things."

I asked, "When do people believe something will be easy?"

"When they know they will be successful."

That was a good answer. Only success itself feels better than the confidence that you will have success.

Would you like that confidence? You will have it when you use the connection builders of the easy way. I will describe those right after we agree on a couple of assumptions.

Two Foundation Piers

Saying hard things the easy way rests on two truths about human nature. It calls to my mind the suspension bridge over the Arkansas River at the Royal Gorge in Colorado. When we look at a suspension bridge, we first notice the long cables, the dramatic element of such a bridge. Their graceful, gentle curves give us no clue of their incredible strength. From a distance the cables look delicate, but they hold the weight.

Most of this book is about connections. It's about "cables" we can use to connect our side of a situation with another person's side so we can have an easy flow of communication and activity.

But if we had only cables, we would not have a suspension bridge. It also needs towers, the other feature of a suspension bridge that we see at first glance. Without towers there's no bridge. These towers usually grow from other features of a suspension bridge that are of equal importance, although in many bridges they are not easily seen. These crucial features are the foundation piers. They must be the most solid of structures for they carry the weight of the entire bridge and whatever is on it.

During construction of the Royal Gorge bridge, the loose, gravely surface soil was dug away down to granite bedrock, then concrete was poured to create the solid piers. These piers aren't glamorous. They probably are not even noticed by most visitors. But without them the bridge would not be there and we would not be able to walk across it and peer over the edge to the roaring river 1,053 feet below.

Like a suspension bridge, saying hard things the easy way rests on two piers of truth about human nature. These truths are: (1) people are interested in taking care of themselves, and (2) people need and want other people in their lives.

Another way to say this is that humans want to be independent *and* interdependent. We want to get along *without* other people, but we also want to be *with* people. These seemingly contradictory impulses arise within each of us. They even exist at the same time.

It's okay that way. When you understand these two urges, you can harness them to move situations toward goals that are good for you. These are foundation piers for the easy way. We will build our connections on them.

The Goal of This Book

The goal of this book is to help you get your needs met. Not to go after what you need is an injustice to yourself and to the people who are important in your life.

Since our goal is for you to meet your needs, it may seem odd that this chapter is about talking with other people about *their* needs. But there's a good reason for this.

The Connection Cables of the Easy Way

The power to talk with people the easy way, and to influence them, comes as you *take genuine interest in their needs*. Your authentic concern for what is best for this person is the roadway across the easy-way bridge.

To understand how interest in the needs of others will help you get your own needs met, think again of the two foundation piers: One pier reminds us that humans selfishly want to be totally independent. If you can help a person get what he or she wants, that person may help you get what *you* want. A fair trade is good for both.

The other pier reminds us that humans want to be interdependent—to be connected with others. If you can unselfishly give to a person you've "connected" with, that is even better than trading favors, for it brings you the joys and benefits of altruism.

You will use these truths as you approach others in quest of getting your needs met. These truths will help you and will build your confidence that you can say hard things the easy way.

The Interests of Others Are Your Interests, Too

You can get your needs met only if you cooperate with other people. We *all* are interdependent, whether we want to be or not.

People cooperate with others when there is something in it for them. *They* will be interdependent with *you* when they see that doing so will help them get their needs met.

So it is in your best interests to take true interest in other people. It will be valuable to you to learn how to understand other people—not to manipulate them, but so you and they can cooperate better. There are two strong reasons why that will be good for both of you.

Reason number one: Your honest interest in their needs may increase their interest in you. Your sincere interest in them is likely to touch something within them that makes them want to take interest in you.

Reason number two: Your interest is what they need. People need people. Most people try many times a day to attract positive attention from others. There aren't very many hermits in the world. Even if we include the thousands of urban hermits (who are surrounded by people but never connect with anyone), there are few humans who do not long to be cared about by others.

Your interest in the other person is the key to comfort and success in many of the awkward situations you face. It will get you "off the hook" and gratify the other person's longings at the same time. That will be especially clear in chapter 4.

This Is Not a Book for Con Artists

Interest in others must be for real. I already have used several words to describe the qualities your interest must have: genuine, true, sincere, honest, and authentic.

If you want to be a phony manipulator, read no further. Being bogus is an insult to yourself and others. It doesn't work.

But if you want to understand people more exactly and completely, read on. Taking an interest in people—honestly and unselfishly—will open the door to more pleasing human relations.

How to Communicate Your Interest in Others

The first technique of the book is called "mirroring." While it is just one communication skill among many, it is one of the most useful. It can be helpful in many different situations.

Some human-relations trainers have been so impressed with it they have taught it as the only skill you need. Not so. But it is an energetic, healthy skill to have in your human-relations tool kit.

Mirroring is sometimes known by other names. It has been called active listening, reflective listening, paraphrasing, and the interchangeable response. I like the term mirroring best because it describes what it does.

When you look in a mirror, you can see yourself more completely than you can without a mirror. Try to see your ears without a mirror, for example! It is easy to learn certain things about yourself with a mirror.

The technique of mirroring is to hold up a "mirror of words" to another person so he or she can understand himself or herself more completely. Again, it reveals things not seen otherwise.

It is very easy to explain how to do mirroring. Perhaps you already use this valuable skill. If not, you will soon learn to use it skillfully and enjoy its benefits. I shall present it here step-by-step.

Content and Feelings

Communication always has two parts: content and feelings. Content is what the person is talking about, and he or she always has feelings about that content. (Sometimes the feelings are not very strong.) It is valuable to us to know about both parts.

How Mirroring Is Done

To mirror other people's experiences, you simply respond with a few words to describe (1) what they have told you about what is happening to them (content), and (2) what they told you about how they feel about it (feelings). Your mirroring response is a summary of what you have heard from them: It adds nothing, and leaves out nothing. Here's how it looks in a diagram:

1. Talker describes
   content and feelings.

2. Listener restates
   the talker's
   content and feelings.

3. The talker is aware
   of being understood
   and accepted.

Here's how it might sound in a short conversation. Bob describes a hassle he had recently, and Rich responds using the technique of mirroring.

BOB: My car conked out the other day. It really made me mad when it quit running.
      [Bob's report of content: car conked out. Bob's report of his feelings: mad.]

RICH: You were pretty disgusted when it wouldn't go. [Rich's mirror image of Bob's content: It wouldn't go. Rich's mirror image of Bob's feelings: disgusted.]

What Happens?

Three good things happen right away:
1. Bob enjoys and appreciates being understood and accepted. That enjoyment begins the building of a bond of trust and caring between Bob and Rich.

2. Because Bob is comfortable, he talks freely. He gives Rich more information than Rich could get by asking questions. Rich doesn't know what questions to ask. But he's learned this principle: "If you want to get to know someone, let him or her tell you. You'll learn more, and learn it faster by listening than by asking questions."

3. Rich begins to understand Bob more completely. We cannot influence a person or a situation without understanding. We can not have understanding without information. We get information by making it easy for the other person to tell us.

We see three quick benefits from one simple skill. Impressive, isn't it?

The Case of Kurt and the Quicksand

This book uses many scripts to illustrate the skills. In these scripts, the person who is using the skill we are studying will be labeled "Easy Way." Just think of Easy Way as an assistant coach who helps me. We'll ask Easy Way to put on a demonstration from time to time. I'll give some play-by-play commentary after each demonstration. Let's do one now.

In this example, Kurt is complaining to Easy Way, who responds with mirroring. As you read what Kurt says, identify his content (what's happening) and his feelings (about the content). Then see if both of these, and nothing more, are in Easy Way's response.

KURT: Three years already, you and I have been working at this place. I only came here as a last resort.

EASY WAY: You were desperate then, so you did it.

KURT: I had to. But it's been downhill every day since.

EASY WAY: That must make it rough to be here.

KURT: Here, and everywhere else.

EASY WAY: It isn't just the job then. Some other things are difficult, too. That's got to be real hard on you now.

(Comment: Notice Kurt's content and feelings mirrored back to him in each of Easy Way's responses. How do we know if that is useful to Kurt or not? We find out by listening to the rest of the conversation to see if Kurt continues, and tells more, or if he gets out of the conversation. Judge for yourself.)

KURT: Yeah. I'm about to disappear in a pit of problems. Money is a big problem. I'm in a ruckus with my best friend. The list goes on.

EASY WAY: From what you say, it must seem to you like your are sinking in quicksand. I don't know if those are things you want me to know about, but if you want to talk about them, I'll listen.

KURT: I need to talk to someone. But there's nothing anyone but me can do.

EASY WAY: It sounds like you want to talk. And I want to listen. Things seem hopeless to you right now, I guess, but maybe they aren't.

KURT: No, maybe they aren't. But, you see, I got this letter from a lawyer saying that I have to. . . .

(Comment: What happened in this conversation? Easy Way proved to be a good listener. Kurt wants to talk more and is ready to trust Easy Way with more personal information.)

Benefits of Mirroring

Mirroring is the smoothest road to a relationship of trust and respect with another person.

Mirroring works best:

1. To begin a relationship of trust and caring.

2. To help other persons understand themselves better.

3. When you find it hard to understand what other persons are saying or you don't know what they mean by what they say. It will help you communicate accurately.

4. When your ideas and the ideas of the other person are quite different. Mirroring will help you keep attention on the ideas, and not get emotionally caught up in the contrasts between you.

5. To fill time when you are not sure what else to say. Most communication styles can be destructive, but it is almost impossible to harm a relationship by using the skill of mirroring. If in doubt—use mirroring to be a good listener and to understand better the person who is talking.

Wrong Turns

Just as a shortcut can make the trip easier, one wrong turn can make it more difficult, even dangerous. In the chapters ahead, a "wrong turn" section will describe ways you might get off the road in each situation, and tell you how to protect yourself from harm.

Here are some common mistakes to avoid when using the method of mirroring:

1. Rushing in to give cheap advice instead of waiting to find out what the person needs and wants.

2. Talking about content only, ignoring feelings.

3. Pulling the attention back on yourself.

4. Being a lazy listener. Good listening takes mental and physical energy. Be as intense in your words and emphasis as the other person is.

5. Sounding like a parrot or a robot. A mirror does not leave anything out or add anything new, but your mirror of words can use different words and expressions that mean the same thing the other person has said. This is one way he or she comes to see the situation more clearly.

6. Using mirroring when it is time to do something else. Mirroring is most valuable early in conversations when you are building trust with the person and learning about his or her situation. Once you know what is going on, you can talk more about yourself (see chapter 3) and confront (see chapter 4), as the situation requires.

When You Try It, You'll Find Out

You may not believe that mirroring is a valuable skill until it is helpful in your own life. I didn't. Years ago, early in my training, I was teaching this skill to others, but I wasn't convinced that it was practical in everyday life.

One evening, just home from the university where I was both teaching and studying, I had settled into my easy chair with the newspaper. My son, then a first-grader, came into the house crying. He stood beside me, his knee skinned raw and bloody, tears streaming down his face.

His content? An injured knee. His feelings? Physical pain and a jumble of emotions that I suppose included frustration, fear, anger, and loneliness (pain is such a solo experience).

He didn't say anything in words, but stood in front of me, wailing. I thought it was a good time to put the mirroring technique to the test. I mirrored his content and feelings.

"Wow!" I said. "You took quite a lick on your knee, there. I'll bet that really hurts!"

Straightening his back and squaring his shoulders, he looked me in the eye and said, "I guess it will be all right." And the tears—trust me—rolled back up his cheeks and disappeared. He walked away and I thought, *it works!*

It still does. It is a handy and valuable tool for me, and it can be for you. I urge you to try it enough to discover in your own experience that it can be useful in your life, too.

The One Difficulty in Learning This Skill

The hardest part in mirroring is keeping the attention on the other person's content and feelings, instead of putting it on ourselves. Most of us would rather control the conversation by asking questions or giving answers. Mirroring does neither of those things.

Summary

Mirroring is a potent communication skill. Use it with honesty and careful thought for your own benefit and for the benefit of those around you. In chapter 6 and following, you will see it applied to many relationship situations.

3

You Can Talk
with People
about
Your Needs and
Feelings

This chapter teaches another powerful skill that is useful in many different types of situations. It is the "I-statement." Much as the skill of mirroring was taught, the fundamentals will be taught first and later chapters will show how the skill can help you fix specific hard problems.

Choose a Vehicle to Fit the Trip

It is easy for other persons to continue talking with you when you give mirroring responses, because mirroring helps you show interest in and respect for them. Mirroring carries no judgment or condemnation. It is gentle in intensity—like riding on a smooth highway in a large car.

Talking about *your* needs, however, may require you to state displeasure with the other person's behavior. That's not so easy for you to say, nor for them to hear. It is not so gentle in intensity. For this "rougher road" we might prefer a sturdy pickup truck.

The I-statement is a vehicle that will carry you through these more intense situations. It will help you say some hard things the easy way.

The I-Statement

An I-statement expresses your genuine thoughts and feelings in response to an event that may be another person's words, attitudes, or actions. This event may lead to positive or negative feelings in you. An I-statement is a brief report of the event and feelings. For example:

- "When you called me a 'sucker,' I felt angry."
- "I feel good when I win at tennis."
- "When you complimented me, I was pleased."
- "I get worried when my bank account is low."
- "If the check comes early, I'll be overjoyed."

An I-statement doesn't include much, does it? It's just a statement of *your feelings* about an *event*.

Think of all it does *not* include: It does not talk about anyone else's feelings. It does not blame, judge, or scold. It does not make any plan for action. It's a report; that's all.

But it may influence another person to change. So, the I-statement is a very gentle way to complain. Because it works quite often, and rarely creates any bad effects, it is a vehicle of communication well worth learning and using.

Let's see how the I-statement might be used. Suppose Dana, a co-worker with whom you often sit at coffee break, has blown cigarette smoke into the face of Pat, another co-worker. It seems to have been done on purpose.

Pat might use the I-statement pattern to report displeasure to Dana. As a first response to what has happened she could say: "Dana, I find that unpleasant," or, "Dana, the smoke is offensive to me. I call it to your attention because, while I like talking with you, I find the smoke irritating," or, "It disappoints me that you seem to be careless about how your smoke affects me."

Will this fix the problem? Maybe. But maybe not, because the I-statement is a very gentle method. I suggest you use it first, and if it doesn't get the results you need, that you move on to more intense methods described in the next chapter.

A Risky Wrong Turn

It is common to want to attack the other person who's being offensive. It's just plain human, actually. A "you-statement" attacks. For example, Pat might have said, "Dana, you are crude, childish, and inconsiderate. I told you before how obnoxious you are. What's the matter with you, you dork?"

This harsh reply has great intensity and will probably only create more anger between the two. Like a wall of fire, it will hold them apart and hurt them both. I expect that you are sympathetic to Pat, as I am, but this response style only makes a bad situation worse.

A Wasteful Wrong Turn

So we reject you-statements. But we like the skill of mirroring. Would it solve the problem here? Let's see.

Pat says, "Dana, you must think it's okay to blow your smoke onto other people, and I guess you're comfortable doing that." There—that's a mirroring response. Does it accomplish anything? No. Mirroring is a communication tool for a different purpose. It deals with the other person's feelings and it does not confront. It does not help the other person know how we feel or think.

More I-Statements

Later, if we thought it would be beneficial, you or I might report to Dana how we are affected by the incident. In I-statement form, we might say one of these sentences:

"Dana, I'm concerned about the attitude you show toward Pat. It looks to me as though your attitude and actions may become harmful to you." Or we might say, "When you blew smoke on Pat the second time today, it seemed to me that it was deliberate. That makes me uneasy, because that's not in the best interests of either of you." Or, "I'm afraid that you might be creating a major problem for yourself by your actions, such as blowing smoke on Pat at coffee break."

These statements report the speaker's feelings about an event—nothing more, nothing less. Compare the I-statements with you-statements and mirroring.

Benefits of I-Statement

The I-statement is a special communication tool that is great for certain jobs. Though gentle, an I-statement can be forceful when used at the right time. It has many benefits.

1. It can be used with positive or negative feelings.

2. It is low risk. You can start gently and increase the intensity.

3. It helps you put the attention on behavior, not on people. It helps you avoid attacking people in personal ways.

4. It may influence another person to change.

5. It is easy, because the formula helps you organize your thoughts.

6. It lets you release your tension, even when the other person does not change behavior.

7. It may help build a bond between people.

The I-statement can be a handy addition to your human-relations tool kit. Let's learn how to do it.

Making I-Statements the Easy Way

All it takes to build an I-statement is an event and a feeling from your own life. Of course, these have something to do with the other persons or you wouldn't be talking with them. You can put the two pieces together in either of these patterns:

"I feel __*(feeling)*__ when __*(event)*__."
"When you __*(event)*__, I felt *(feeling)*."

We can talk about the past or the future, too.

"I felt __*(feeling)*__ when __*(event)*__."
"I will feel __*(feeling)*__ if __*(event)*__."

These patterns will guide you when you plan and rehearse how you will fix some obstacles in your life. You may wish to write I-statements about your situation as a way of organizing your thoughts. Later, in your real-life conversation, you'll be able to get the message across in your own regular style. The pattern will help you get ready.

The I-Statement As a Confrontation

An I-statement lets you talk about what you need and how you feel. It begins with *your* goals, not the goals of the other person. The other person may not care about what you need. The more important you are to the other person, the more likely he or she will take the hint from the I-statement—and change.

If your feelings are not important, he or she probably won't change. If it works, fine; it not, no harm is done. Then you decide whether to let it go or use more intense methods.

The Sources of Our Feelings

People often believe their feelings are caused by other persons. We hear remarks such as "You make me angry," "You hurt my feelings," or "It's all your fault that I'm so upset." But the truth is that other persons do not have that type of direct power over us.

While it *is* true that our feelings are *influenced* by the behavior of others, the connection between the behavior of other people and our feelings is not direct. We have much more opportunity to influence our feelings than they do.

The influence other people have on my life begins with my perception of what they do. That is, I find out about it: I see it, hear about it, or read about it. In some way I take note of it. This is my first chance for error, because I may not get the facts straight. I may respond to information that is false.

After I perceive the event, I think about it. This offers a second chance for error because I may use faulty thinking at this point. If I am mistaken about how the world works, my emotional response may be incorrect. Suppose I am an American driving a car in England. As I cruise along on the right-hand side of a lovely, two-lane road in a remote part of the country, an oncoming car approaches—on my side of the road. I panic. "That idiot is driving on the wrong side of the road! We're going to crash!" I shriek. In this example, my perception was okay. The other driver was on the same side of the road as I was. But my thinking was faulty. The other driver wasn't on the wrong side—I was. Bad feelings often come from such faulty thinking.

Sometimes events jump into our awareness and we think about them whether we want to or not. These events will trigger feelings, whether we want them to or not. To show how this might happen, I'll describe a rather far-fetched example—but one that shows how feelings can quickly emerge this way. If you see a goat with an owl riding on its back wandering around outside your house, you are sure to start thinking about the goat and the owl. You're thinking about a goat and an owl right now, aren't you? You see them in your mind.

If the goat and the owl were, in fact, outside your window, you would have feelings—surprise and bewilderment among them, no doubt. You would be curious about where they came from, who they belonged to, and so on. You hadn't planned to think about a goat and an owl, but you did. Unexpected thoughts jump into our minds many times a day.

Suppose you are standing at the window watching the goat and the owl, and three roaring tigers leap into the room with you. Boom! You perceive, you think, and in less time than it takes to read the word terrorized, you are. Does it matter that between the tigers' coming in and your feelings, you perceived and thought? Not in this case.

But in many situations it will be worthwhile for you to run the situation back in super slow motion to find out what your thoughts were, because the quality of the feelings will be only as good as the quality of the thoughts. Incorrect thoughts lead to incorrect feelings. Exaggerated thoughts to exaggerated feelings. Crummy thoughts to crummy feelings.

You can depend on these statements about the nature of feelings:

1. It is not constructive to blame other persons for your feelings.

2. Your feelings are likely to be out of order if your perception is distorted.

3. Your feelings are your responsibility, not the responsibility of others.

4. Your feelings can change by changing how and what you think.

I-statements help you sort out your feelings. As you organize your thoughts and feelings you will understand yourself better and express yourself better to others.

Changing the Intensity of I-Statements

The intensity of an I-statement can be changed two ways. One way is by the choice of words. Notice in the examples below how the intensity grows as you read down the list.

- "When you insulted me I felt surprised."
- "When you insulted me I felt a little annoyed."
- "When you insulted me I felt irritated."
- "When you insulted me I felt sort of upset."

- "When you insulted me I felt disgusted."
- "When you insulted me I felt angry."

A second way to make an I-statement more intense is by changing your tone of voice and other nonverbal modes. A statement is less intense when your voice is "matter of fact" and your gestures are slow and undramatic. It becomes more intense as you give your voice an edge of urgency or anger, or as you speak louder or faster. It becomes even more intense as you get physically closer to the other person and as gestures are more emphatic.

Summary

An I-statement is useful (1) as a gentle confrontation, (2) to give or receive a compliment, (3) to let the other person know you more fully, or (4) to relieve your tension. It is a simple, but powerful, vehicle that can help you move past many situations.

The pickup truck of the I-statement is dandy for rough gravel roads, but sometimes we need to get off the road and through some very rough terrain. In the next chapter we will drive a stronger vehicle, confrontation, which will carry us past tougher obstacles.

4

You Can Talk with People about What They Need to Change

Larry tells you something on Monday and swears it's the truth. On Thursday he says the opposite of what he said on Monday. He insists that this, too, is the truth.

Marie could do well in her sales job but is not trying. She faults the customers, the economy, and the weather. She blames her poor performance on everything except her own lack of effort.

Ned says he will quit smoking today. It seems you have heard him say that three hundred times. Even as he says it now, he is buying cigarettes.

Confrontation

In each of these cases two things contradict each other: what Larry says Monday and what he says Thursday, Marie's excuses and reality, Ned's vow and what he does. When you tell a person two parts of his or her life are in conflict with each other, that is a confrontation.

One meaning of the word confrontation is "an incident of hostility or opposition between people." We will not use it in that sense. Here we use confrontation in its other meaning: "to bring together face-to-face for examination or comparison." Again, there is an opposition (or conflict or discrepancy), but it is between behaviors, attitudes, or beliefs.

Taking Two Roads at Once

Living with such an opposition within one's life is like trying to drive down two roads at once. An accident is bound to happen soon, but people live this way a lot. The reason they do is that they have not chosen between two directions. For example, Ned is motivated to quit smoking because he wants to stay healthy, but he also is motivated to keep on smoking by physical addiction. He hasn't chosen a direction, so he says one thing and does another.

Marie is motivated to have high sales by the money and recognition it would bring her. On the other hand, she may be motivated to *not* try to make sales because she fears if she tries she will fail. Larry has his own secret agendas, and we may not be able to learn what they are. There are other reasons people allow discrepancies in their lives. They may be confused or lack complete information. They may change their minds about what they want. Or, if they are trying to live a lie, they may lose track of what they are telling people. The discrepancy we hear from Larry might be explained by any of these.

Confronting such people is sometimes necessary. There are many times at home, work, and elsewhere when you need to be able to confront others. You can learn to do it well. Confrontation the easy way involves the five components listed below. We shall look at each of these components in the following sections.

1. *Assumptions:* what confrontation is and how it works
2. *A starting point*: a relationship for confrontation
3. *A map:* strategy for the process
4. *Vehicles*: a range of intensity
5. *Timing:* knowing when to confront

Assumptions

Before we get to the actual techniques, let's consider some basic assumptions about confrontation that will give us courage—and insight—for what we're doing.

1. *Confrontation is an act of caring.* The confronter is not willing for the other person to live with an internal discrepancy that may harm him or her. The confronter will not sit quietly by, watching the person walk blindly toward a cliff.

2. *Confrontation is a responsibility.* Confrontations we have received from others have helped us grow in wisdom and self-control. We ought to give others the same benefit.

3. *Confrontation puts limits on the relationship.* It states that we do not fully accept something about the other person's behavior, beliefs, or attitudes. To some extent we reject part of the other person. This can be painful to him or her and scary for you because you wonder if you may be rejected in return.

4. *Confrontation must be an act of integrity.* Because entering into another person's life is risky, doing it can be motivated only out of selfishness—or out of love. The confronted person will quickly know from which motive it comes. Confrontation must resist dirtying the relationship with snobbery or spite. It must know the difference between punishment and discipline, right and wrong, justice and mercy.

5. *Confrontation seeks to help other persons know themselves better.* The confronter does as much as possible to understand before trying to teach understanding.

6. *Confrontation must be done with care and flexibility.* It may take some brute force to move entrenched habits into new directions, but at the same time, it needs finesse. Humans are fragile and can be painfully broken. So the confronter decides whether to be direct or indirect, to confront now or later, to be gentle or tough. The vehicle of confrontation can be a limousine, a pickup truck, or a car-crushing monster truck.

7. *Confrontation is an act of courage.* It may strain the relationship for a time. The confronter may be ignored, rebuffed, ridiculed, attacked—or all of these. The confronter recognizes and accepts the risk and tries to keep it to a minimum.

8. *Confrontation is an investment in the future.* There may not be any benefit for a long time. In the short run it is easier to avoid the hassle and not confront, but that's a second-best choice.

9. *Confrontation is an uncomfortable act for many persons.* Knowing that the confronted person might be a little tense often creates tension in the confronter. But avoiding or postponing usually makes it more difficult to do later.

10. *Confrontation is an act of optimism.* The confronter becomes deeply involved in the life of the other person by challenging that person to become more involved in his or her own life. It is the confronter's way of saying, "Life is good. It is so good that I'm not willing for you to half-live your life."

Starting Point

People who know you care about them are more likely to listen to and think about what you say. If they trust and respect you, and you trust and respect them, confrontation is more likely to be helpful. So the starting point for successful confrontation is to build a relationship of trust and respect. Mirroring helps greatly with that.

Confrontation puts something new into the other persons' lives: a truth we believe they need to consider. They may not want it. The truth hurts. We show Marie, the sales representative, that she is blaming the weather—or the economy or the customers—for the results of her own laziness. She may not be interested in hearing that. It is even likely to be quite unpleasant to her.

When we point out to Larry that his Monday and Thursday statements don't match up, he may say, "What right do you have to butt into my life this way?"

If we have a respectful, trusting relationship with Larry and Marie, confronting about these problems is likely to be less painful and more helpful.

A Map

On what occasions do you confront? Your map, or plan, will tell you when to make turns and when to stop. It will also give you guidelines for when to proceed. You have the right to proceed with a confrontation when you are being harmed by the action of others.

You have the right—and the duty—to confront a friend. As friendship develops, you and your friend give each other permission to tell it like it is when that is good for you.

You have the right to confront when another person is seeking your advice about his or her situation and when you are in a position of authority over or responsibility for the other. This includes, among others, the roles of parent, employer, and supervisor.

The Vehicles of Confrontation

Chapter 3 gave the concept of the gentle-to-tough range of confrontations. The I-statement is the most gentle form of confrontation. We noted that it may be forceful enough, especially when confronting a person who cares about how you feel.

The skills taught in this chapter are more intense than I-statements. They help you continue to treat the other person with respect but recognize that at times you may have to be firm, or even pushy, to make change happen.

Since the goal of confrontation is to get other persons to change, you will not want to displease them more than necessary. Usually the best plan is to start with gentle intensity and raise the intensity as required. If you can get their cooperation without much force, great! If you have to shift into low gear and use four-wheel drive, that's the way it must be.

In chapter 1 we said that the techniques for overcoming obstacles were like cars that could take us through the plan, or map, we had devised. The technique in this discussion is confrontation. We'll look at four different vehicles that represent the range of intensities that occur in confrontations: weak, gentle, tough, and harsh. We'll also look at a technique I call "leaving the car with the motor running." The weak and harsh extremes listed below are more likely to be harmful than helpful. But we'll look at them because it is easy to slip into using them and it's important to recognize them when they occur. These examples portray a person talking to a friend.

A Car That Won't Run

First, the weak style. "I probably shouldn't say this, 'cause it's not really my place to say anything about it. It's about your job, so it's something you're probably already thinking about anyway. But, uh, it seems like you get to work late a lot. Well, like I said, it's none of my business. So, just forget I said anything about it."

A weak confrontation won't get you any further than a wrecked car in a junk yard. It is so flimsy in its message or in the style with which it is said that the other person doesn't pay attention to it. At best, it's in one ear and out the other.

Such weakness may even lead the confronted person to lose respect for you. He or she may assume you don't believe in what you are talking about or don't have the guts to speak up for your beliefs. An extremely weak confrontation may even be interpreted as approval of the behavior, as if you had said, "I think what you are doing is okay, but I am obligated to talk to you about it. Go ahead with things as they are, but try to keep it quiet."

Weak confrontations are usually a sign of fear. This may come from lack of confidence in the message itself or in one's ability to justify it.

The Tank

The opposite extreme is a confrontation so harsh it is damaging to the other person. "The way you get to work so late, you ought to be ashamed of yourself. You're lucky they haven't fired you, which is what I would do if you worked for me. Not that I would hire such a sack rat."

A harsh confrontation is so disrespectful in what it says or in the way in which is it said that it is almost sure to hurt the relationship. The harsh confrontation is a vehicle of war: It shows no respect; it protects no one. Instead, it points out minor faults, beats the other person over the head with blame, and runs the risk of blowing things out of proportion.

The nonverbal style has a lot of frenzy and noise. It sometimes makes threats.

The result is a wall of mistrust and dislike between the two people. The confronted person will probably stay away from the confronter, get angry and go on the attack, or pretend to accept the information but ignore it later.

This kind of confrontation is generally given by confronters who are frustrated and hostile about their own lives. It may give them a brief sense of power or release of tension. But in the long run, harsh confrontations are even more destructive to the giver than to the receiver.

The Off-Road 4 x 4

Now that we've seen the two extremes of confrontation—weak and harsh—let's look at the gentle and tough intensities in between.

If a weak confrontation is like a junker that won't run and the harsh confrontation is like a tank, the gentle confrontation is a heavy-duty vehicle, like a four-wheel drive pick-up or Bronco. It can tour the city streets with ease and comfort, but is ready to go through the forest and across the streams and gullies when it needs to.

Gentle confrontations are likely to be effective. They have enough intensity to be taken seriously by the other person without pushing him or her into a corner. Example: "You mentioned that in most ways your performance on the job is very good. They like you there. But it makes your boss unhappy for people to come late. Many times one major flaw—like coming in late—is enough to spoil the chance for a promotion to something better. That might be something for you to think about."

Here are secrets to gentle confrontation:

1. *Generalize.* Talk about people in general instead of just the other person. For example, "Lots of people find out that if they don't treat others with respect they don't get treated well themselves." This is a hint. The other person can take it personally or not.

2. *Use "loophole" words.* Loophole words soften the blow because it is easy for the other person to wiggle out of the confrontation if he or she isn't ready to deal with it. For example, "It sounds like *now and then* you get *a little* annoyed with her and you *almost wish* you could *sort of* get even." That's a lot less intense than saying, "You're mad at her and want revenge!" Another example could add, "That *might* be something for you to think about."

3. *Use humor.* This is more likely to fit in when the other person is asking for help, than it will in a disciplinary case.

4. *Build a relationship first.* The more mutual trust and caring you share with the other person, the better it will go. If you can, take all the time you need to listen and understand him or her before you confront.

5. *Use nonverbal style.* Be relaxed and confident. Use a tone of voice that carries both your caring and your concern. Have regular eye contact.

6. *Be flexible.* Allow for the possibility that you may not be seeing things the way they really are. Nudge the persons you're confronting; don't try to tie them up and run away with them.

Gentle confrontations have several strengths: (1) They are less risky than tough confrontations, (2) they bring out less resistance, and (3) they are easier to deliver.

The "Mudder"

Now our confrontation gets really intense. We take our basic 4 x 4 vehicle, lift the body, put 44-inch tires on it, customize it in other ways, and it becomes one mean machine. We're ready to race in the mud or barge through whatever is in the way. This represents confrontation of tough intensity: a specialized vehicle suitable for just a few places, capable of a lot of damage if uncontrolled, useful but dangerous.

As you put more emphasis on the negative parts, the experience becomes more intense both for you, giving the confrontation, and for the person hearing it. But you continue to communicate with great care and respect. Example: "You've told me when you were late for work today it was the third time in the last eight days, and your boss is rather unhappy about it. You said you are worried about it. It's a step in the right direction to worry about it. But you need to do more than that. You say you're serious about fixing the problem. Great! What is your plan? How will you be sure to get to work on time tomorrow?"

These guidelines can be compared with the guidelines for gentle confrontations. Match them up, number for number.

1. *Personalize.* Make it clear you are talking about the other person.

2. *Specify events.* Be clear what you are talking about. Pin it down so the person must accept or reject what you say. Point out examples of the person's actions. Quote the person, as above, "You've told me. . . ." and "You say. . . ." The confrontation becomes more intense when we describe consequences that will befall the person if he or she does not change or conform to necessary expectations. This is called an ultimatum.

3. *Be somber.* In words and nonverbal style, create an atmosphere of seriousness about the situation. If more than one person is doing the confronting, it is a lot more intense.

4. *Cash in on the relationship.* Point out the cost to the other person if the relationship between the two of you is damaged by his or her failure to make needed changes. Does this

sound like putting him or her on a guilt trip? Yes, one that's done for his or her good.

5. *Use an urgent nonverbal style.* Your voice will carry more concern and urgency. Although you may be confronting the person because you care a lot about him or her, you may not sound congenial. Your desire to do what is best in the situation overrides your desire to be comfortable.

6. *Be persistent.* You will not get off the track. A series of gentle confrontations becomes a tough confrontation. Ask how the person will take care of what needs to be done. You might ask, "What is your plan? What are you going to do about it? Exactly when will you do that?"

Leaving the Car with the Motor Running

If I confront you and you don't like it, it is easy to get away from me. But if you confront yourself, where do you go to get away from it? A gentle remark may be a seed that does not sprout for a few days or weeks. But when it does sprout, it may be well noticed and lead to great change in the person.

One of the nicest things we can do for other people, and it can help us a great deal, too, is to put a confrontation where they will take it on their own. We sort of park a good car in plain sight, leave the motor running, and walk away from it, hoping they will get in and drive away. It's super when it works. Sometimes it is all we can do. We couldn't drag some people an inch with the biggest tow truck in the world, but if we give them a way to travel on their own, they'll take it.

Timing

It is often a lot easier to know *how* to confront than to know *when*. The right time, of course, is when the other person is ready to accept and act upon the information we're sharing. Here are some other hints about timing.

Confront:

1. When you need to protect a person from his or her own actions, or to protect others. To say, "Don't do that!" is still right and proper; it is merely unpopular.

2. When a person is showing progress in some areas of life but not in others. Confrontation to this blocked area may help the person move on.

3. When someone is mildly confronting himself or herself. Self-confrontation is an act of strength you can praise; you can support the person's resolve to change.

Do not confront:

1. When it would hurt more than benefit. For example, do not point out discrepancies the person cannot change.

2. When you have a "holier-than-thou" attitude.

3. Because someone else wants you to, but you're not convinced it needs to be done.

4. Before you understand the person and his or her situation fairly well.

Yet sometimes a confrontation shot from the hip is beneficial, as reported in this newspaper story: A twenty-seven-year-old man weighing 435 pounds was eating in a restaurant when a stranger approached and asked how old he was. "Old enough to know better," the obese man replied.

The stranger scolded, "A young man like you shouldn't allow himself to be that fat!" The stranger's remark stung, but it shocked the overweight man into action. During the next eight months he lost 210 pounds.

The hard, straight confrontation from a stranger was useful. Information and pleas from friends, physician, and family had not motivated him. This did. It went against the guidelines. It was a like monster truck that spun its wheels and splattered mud on the man to get his attention; it was risky, but it worked. If the guy couldn't have tolerated the statement, we would have to categorize it as harsh. Prudent, caring people will start gently, raising the intensity little by little, and as they do they will carefully observe the effect on the person who's being confronted.

Almost always it is best to build strong trust before you confront. Start gentle, then raise the intensity little by little, as you need to.

Examples of Varying Intensity

The statements below illustrate the four levels of intensity. These are confrontations to a high-school boy who says he wants a part-time job but who is not looking for one.

Ineffective Confrontations (because they are weak):

1. "Jobs are pretty hard to get." (This excuses the boy for not looking.)
2. "It takes a lot of looking to find a job these days." (True, but so what?)

Effective Confrontations (ranging from gentle to tough):

3. "I'm sort of surprised you're not finding a job." (Very gentle I-statement)
4. "I'm disappointed you're not looking for a job." (Another I-statement)
5. "It would be neat for you to have a part-time job. You will probably need to do a lot of looking in order to find one." (Affirmation and advice)
6. "I guess it is going to take a lot of time making applications here and there in order to find a job." (Information)
7. "I've heard you say you want to get a part-time job, but I haven't heard you say anything about going out to look." (Reports the discrepancy without comment)
8. "You talk about getting a job, but you have not been applying for jobs. It makes me wonder how strongly you mean what you say about wanting one. If you're serious about getting a job, you'll need to be out looking for it. What are you planning to do?" (Points out a discrepancy, interprets the discrepancy, and asks for a plan)
9. "You say you want to get a job, but you just loaf around the house all day. You complain, but you don't do anything.

When are you going to get off your duff, go out and knock on doors, and find yourself a job?" (Personal opinions are strongly and bluntly expressed. A plan is described with the demand to know when it will be used.)

Ineffective, and probably damaging confrontation (because it is harsh):
   10. "What's the matter with you? You think that someone is going to pop out of the TV set with a job for you? You're acting like a lazy slob, doing nothing but feeling sorry for yourself and driving me crazy with your complaining. You should be as ambitious as the boy next door." (It may all be true, but is saying it in this way helpful or harmful?)

Summary

   Confrontation need not be hard. Prepare the way by taking genuine interest in the needs of the other person. The skill of mirroring will help with that. Start with gentle confrontation and become more intense as necessary.

   Prepare ahead of time by organizing your thoughts. This will build your confidence. Talk it out with a friend. (You're not going to write and deliver a speech, but the preparation will benefit you at the time you are one-to-one with the other person!)

   Now you've been exposed to some strong, generic skills. But it's one thing to know what to do and another to do it. Next, consider how to remove the barriers and gain the power to do what you need to do.

5

You Can Have Power to Do What You Need to Do

One evening I watched a man, prominent in his community, give a presentation before an audience of forty-five hundred people. He walked casually about the stage as he talked, seemingly relaxed and confident. His delivery seemed effortless, yet held the attention of all. He appeared in total command of himself and of the occasion. Judging by the applause, the others in attendance were also impressed and grateful for the information and inspiration he gave.

A couple of nights later his wife phoned me, reporting that while driving to the appearance the man had been so distraught she was afraid he would wreck the car. He was crying, she said, and wailing such things as "I can't do it. I'm scared. I don't know what to say. I'll make a mess of things."

On the way home his condition was, if anything, worse, she said. She told me that he again cried relentlessly, and said, "I did terribly. It didn't go well at all. I can never do anything like that again."

Things Aren't Always the Way They Seem

We in the audience thought the man was comfortable. He wasn't.

He thought he couldn't do it. He did. He thought he hadn't done well. He had.

Sometimes we're wrong about what we can do. *Often,* we are wrong about that.

You can do much more than you have told yourself you can do. Let me just share some ideas, and you can put them in your mind, and then you'll discover whether there is some life-changing truth for you in these thoughts. I'm going to park the car in front of you with the motor running, and you can drive it to a better place if you want.

A Proposition

My belief is that you (and I) often do not see our circumstances accurately and that we exaggerate the obstacles we bump into. We think they are larger, more dangerous, and more difficult to move past than they really are. As a result, we are handicapped by unnecessary fear, and this burden makes our lives more difficult than they need be. We miss out on some of life's goodies because we are hiding from our fears.

But even though I give this little nudge (to us both) I wish us to take note of two other things about our living with fear: (1) So's almost everyone else, including some people we would least expect, such as the guy who looked fantastic on the stage— to everyone but himself. (2) We don't hafta. You don't hafta. I don't hafta—and *I ain't gonna!* What about you?

Remove the Barriers

We have space in this book to give only the basics on how to remove the barriers that have made it hard to move past the obstacles. I'm dividing the problem into three major fears that are keeping millions of people in the garage of life instead of out on the adventure road. In each case, I'll give you the best "fear busters" I know to help you break the ropes of fear so you can head forward on the highway of hope.

But first, promise yourself this: Don't, not even once, scold yourself for the pain your fearfulness has brought you. Learn what you need to learn about your bad habits, but don't punish yourself. Just change. Move ahead. Because *you can.*

Fear of Rejection

An obstacle we encounter as we move along our road may be someone else's pet project. We're rolling along the road when suddenly we have to come to a screeching halt because Lucky Longfellow is camping out with his family and they are conducting a weeny roast and a volleyball game in the middle of the highway.

How do we react? Some people "gun it" and roar right on through while we less courageous folks stand aside and look awe-struck.

For you and me (and almost everyone), it may not be so easy to know what to do. Facing an obstacle, we probably have two motivations: (1) to be nice and easy to get along with, and (2) to push forward toward our own goals. While this discrepancy is uncomfortable, it is very common.

It's understandable that we don't want to be rejected. But when that fear starts creeping in, we should consider two things:

First, who's going to get rejected? If we are blocked from getting our needs met by another person's actions (or lack of action), and we fail to do everything reasonable to reach our goal, we are rejecting ourselves! And that's hard to live with!

If I reject you, no problem. It's easy for you to live without me—you've done it for years. But if *you* reject *you,* where are you going to go to forget about it? That rejection will follow you everywhere.

Rejecting yourself, by failure to act reasonably and vigorously toward healthy personal goals, is costly. Don't do it.

And second, when we are firm with other people, with genuine respect and consideration for them, we almost always get our way. If we don't get all we want, as happens occasionally, time and time again we will come close enough that the difference doesn't matter.

We don't know that, perhaps, because we've backed off too early so many times. Well, you're not going to make that mistake anymore, so you'll learn what Mark Twain learned about needless worry. "I've had thousands of tragedies in my life," he said, "and most of them never happened."

Fear of Fumbling

It can be a long way from the book to "real life," can't it? It's one thing for me to tell you how easy it is and another for you to do it. I know that. I know how hard it can be to put into practice the simple little things discussed in this book, because when it's *my* "real life" I'm emotionally involved, just as you are when it's for you.

Sure, it can be tough to deal with fears. Another common fear is that in the process of confrontation or apologizing or some other task we will get tongue-tied and awkward, and won't look and sound all polished and together. We worry we will stammer instead of being glib, slick, and a model of self-confidence.

When we think that way, we're just being typically human. But the heart of it is pride, and it's a gigantic mistake to let ourselves be ruled by that!

You can kick that bogus concern out of your way. First, recognize that in one-to-one influence, while a smooth delivery is more fun, it isn't what counts. Honesty and common sense do count. *Those* you have, don't you? Sure! You're not up for an Oscar, you're in the conversation to get a job done and you can do it.

Second, with a bit of planning and rehearsal, you're going to be far more polished than you ever thought. Not that it matters, because it doesn't, but you will say what you need to say clearly and convincingly. You'll do it.

Third—and this is super important—who is calling the shots? Is your behavior going to be guided by your desire to avoid the other person's disdain (which is probably not going to be there anyway) or by your desire to obtain your own objectives? Keep yourself as caretaker over your life; don't give the job to someone else.

Fear of Stressors

Don't we get comfortable with the familiar, whether we're really comfortable or not? But a fur-lined rut is still a rut; a cozy mouse nest is still a mouse nest. Don't settle for too little just because you are fearful about the stresses of action and change.

Here are some techniques to keep stress to a minimum and to help cope with the tensions of dealing with sticky problems. Consider these, and use the ones that appeal most to you.

1. Have an escape hatch—an emergency door or a "Plan B"—for getting out of the conversation or for negotiating a settlement of the situation.

2. For conversations that may be controversial, choose a time that is good for the other person. For example, is he or she more relaxed on the weekend than during the week, or would the intrusion on a weekend cause resentment? This is consistent with our commitment to not disrupt the other person's life needlessly.

3. At what time are you most comfortable?

4. What location will be most relaxing? Meeting at a coffee shop might work well. A snack might put you both in a better mood and being in public view would help you both keep conversation moderate and constructive.

5. On the other hand, for many things you don't need that kind of time—sixty seconds or less can accomplish wonders.

6. Rehearsing the conversation with another person is a great confidence builder.

7. One of the tried-and-true relaxers is to slowly take a deep breath, hold it a couple of seconds, and then release it slowly. Repeat this at a leisurely pace five times. Just think! You can do this anywhere. No equipment needed, not even batteries.

8. Reward yourself. If the challenge is great, make the reward worthwhile.

9. Draw power from God. While I think it's quite exciting that God created us with the capacities to run some projects from the power of our little built-in generators, the really great things call for more power than that. So, it's even more exciting to me to know that we can each "wire up" to God's unlimited source of power.

Access the Power

As a psychologist, I'm interested in how people get the way they are. Even more important to me is helping them get to a better place in life, for they deserve that and that is why they have wanted counseling.

In counseling with people I cannot leave out what I believe to be the most important (and only *essential)* part of life: a relationship with God. For the same reason I am unwilling to write this book without stating, simply and concisely, that I believe relationship with God can be real for you and can change your life.

Here, in a few words, are the reasons I believe that knowing God through belief in Jesus Christ is the best thing you can experience:

The evidence of history. Millions of people over thousands of years have attested to newness of life that began with belief in the claims of the Holy Bible.

The Bible's proven reliability. It is practical as an "owner's manual" for life. It's not a book, it's a collection of sixty-six books, and I don't begin to understand them all. But I find that the Bible describes life the way it is, and I find its words to be true.

Observations of and reports from hundreds of people with whom I have counseled. When they have tested the claims of the Bible in their lives, the result has been positive changes in attitude, emotion and relational style so remarkable as to be almost beyond belief. I have seen these changes in them, and their family members and friends have reported seeing them, too. Again and again, these changes have gone far beyond that which secular psychology says is possible. And any explanation other than biblical requires more faith in secular theories than I could ever have. I find the Bible easier to believe than psychological theory. It makes more sense. It answers more questions. It gives more thorough explanations than any other system I've been exposed to. In God's design, the scheme of things seems more congruent, simpler, more complete than psychological theories or secular data. The Bible says we may expect our lives to be transformed as we conform to the plans of our designer. And that's exactly what I've seen happen again and again.

Personal experience. The quality of my own life has been in direct proportion to my obedience to God's design, as described in the Bible.

Jesus Christ, the most exciting person who ever lived! When Jesus was born, shepherds saw the sky filled with angels and rushed to worship him. Wise men saw a star and traveled for months to bring gifts. The jealous king had his army hunting to kill Jesus, but Joseph and Mary escaped with him to a foreign country. After return from exile, the child Jesus astounded the premier religious teachers in Jerusalem with his wisdom and perplexed his parents. Most kids can only do one of those things!

His impact on individuals was so great that men walked off the job to follow him, a woman ran to her village to tell about him, a stingy tax collector gave half his possessions to the poor, a prostitute gave up her trade.

He was so popular he had to disappear from crowds to get peace and quiet, yet he found time to play with children and to be with his friends.

He was unpopular with the religious leaders—and why not? He saw through their hypocrisy; they knew he was right and they couldn't stand it. They set trap after trap to catch him violating religious law and they got caught in their own traps every time. They put a contract out on him.

He was tough. He drove profiteers out of the temple with a whip. When his hypocritical accusers mocked him, beat him, and spit on him, he let dignity and self-control speak for him. When, nailed to the timbers of the cross, he was ridiculed, he could have stepped off the cross and the amazed crowd would have idolized him. He was too strong to cop out, and his strength was spelled l-o-v-e because he was dying to take the penalties that you and I deserve.

There was confusion about his identity. Some thought he was Moses, some thought he was Elijah, some thought he was a con artist ex-carpenter from Nazareth. A few understood that he was the Son of God. But *all knew he was different.*

Amazing things happened. Four men broke through the roof of a house to get their friend close to Jesus for healing. Demons he cast from a naked wild man entered a large herd of pigs and the entire herd—two thousand pigs—rushed into the sea and drowned. Pretty spectacular! Yet John wrote that "Jesus did many other things as well. If every one of them were written down, I suppose that even the whole world would not have room for the books that would be written" (John 21:25). Jesus did things!

He was powerful enough to walk on water and to calm a storm, yet humble enough to wash the feet of his disciples.

None of my friends could feed five thousand people even if they had a mobile grocery store with them. Jesus did it with a borrowed handful of rolls and fish.

He astonished people by knowing their secret attitudes. He so captivated people that they thronged the streets in a massive, spontaneous celebration, laying their garments on the streets for his colt to walk on, waving palm branches and shouting praises.

He healed crippling diseases. Jesus gave sight to the blind and raised the dead—yes, raised the dead!

But this amazes me more: He forgave the soldiers who were killing him and he forgave the crowd that demanded his death, the fickle people who would have crowned him king a few days earlier.

Jesus was exciting!

Jesus is still exciting! He broke out of the tomb; he's alive and he loves you and me. We have crucified him with our own rejection, but he has forgiven us!

Knowing about Jesus is exciting, but knowing *about* him isn't enough. We can *know him personally*. Because Jesus rose from the dead and lives today, his biography continues to be written, and it will include his friendship with you if you want it. I hope you do.

This personal experience with the Christian faith is not just with precepts, but with the person of Christ. To the extent that any of us wants it, Jesus becomes a real hour-by-hour companion. So you and I can have the same experience as the apostle Paul, who said, "I no longer live, but Christ lives in me" (Gal. 2:20).

From the inspiration of personal relationship, from the guidance of principles, and by the comfort and empowerment of the Holy Spirit, living as a Christian is radically different than going through life detached from the Creator. I encourage you to discover and nurture a personal relationship with God through faith in and friendship with Jesus Christ.

6

You Can Put
It All Together
As Well As
Steve Did

We've examined some techniques—vehicles of communication and persuasion—and taken them out for "test drives," one by one. Now let's see what it can be like when the whole fleet is on the job. We'll see the whole convoy of communication skills working together in a dialogue between Steve and Carl.

This conversation was done as a simulation during a workshop in counseling skills. It is fictional, though based on personal experiences. While I don't claim that it proves how things will work in "real life," Steve's confrontation of Carl does illustrate beautifully how "gentle" vehicles such as warmth, caring, and concern can be combined effectively with the "tough" vehicles of confrontation, warning, and ultimatum.

I use this example because it has been helpful to hundreds of men and women in training sessions I have conducted. As a teaching method, it is tried and true. I think it will teach you a lot, too.

The script has not been polished. The stammers, pauses, and awkward sentence constructions are transcribed just as they were spoken, and left in for good reason: Our effectiveness arises from integrity, consideration of the other person, and sensible attention to the issues at hand. Being a "silver-tongued orator" might be nice, but in the whole scheme of things it is not much more significant than a pinstripe on the side of a car—decorative, but it doesn't make the car run any stronger.

As you read, notice the methods Steve uses. Expect to see the vehicles you've studied in this book: mirroring, I-statements, and confrontation.

The purpose of confrontation is to obtain some sort of change. Does Steve state his needs and desires clearly enough for Carl to understand? What effect do Steve's words have on Carl? Does it appear, at the end, that Carl has agreed to make the necessary changes? Are Steve and Carl still on good terms with one another? Read to get these general impressions.

In this situation, Carl is an R.A. (residence assistant) in a large university dormitory who works under Steve's supervision. (Steve and Carl were, at the time, working as college dormitory directors, so they chose that setting for their conversation.) The location they are in and the situation they discuss do not matter. Our interest is in the processes Steve uses, the way he puts them together, and—most of all—the effect Steve's style has on Carl. The numbers following each part of the dialogue correspond to the discussion in the next section.

Steve Confronts Carl

The day before this conversation, Steve had been told that Carl had been seen smoking marijuana with some of the students on his floor. Carl comes to Steve's office to report a maintenance problem, and knocks on the door.

STEVE: Come on in. (1)

CARL: Yeah, Steve. (2)

STEVE: Hi, Carl. (3)

CARL: What do you say? (4)

STEVE: Oh, not much. How you doing, bud? (5)

CARL: This is just a maintenance report on that toilet up on second floor. (6)

STEVE: Good. (7)

CARL: You know, I took care of it, so no problems. (8)

STEVE: Fine. Thanks a lot. (9)

CARL: Yeah. (10)

STEVE: Umm. Now that I've got you here, I want to know, you got a few minutes? I want to talk with you about something. (11)

CARL: Sure. What's up? (12)

STEVE: Well, I'll tell you, uh, I got a report yesterday that kind of disturbed me. And it has to do with you, so I wanted to tell you about it—I want to be real up-front with you—so that you can respond to me and tell me how factual it is. Okay? (13)

CARL: Sure. (14)

STEVE: It came from a person in the building who claims he saw you last week, uh, smoking marijuana with a couple of guys up on your floor, and the reason I ask about that is I just want to have your response to that. (15)

CARL: You're not serious, are you? (16)

STEVE: Yeah, I'm very serious. (17)

CARL: Oh, my heart. Uh . . . I don't know. I don't really feel it's all that fair if I say anything before you tell me who that is. (18)

STEVE: Well, I don't think it's important that you know who it is, frankly, Carl. The important thing is the truth in the matter and that's all I'm concerned about. If somebody's spreading a rumor about you that's not true, I'm going to stop it and I'm going to stop it for good and I can go to the person and clear it up. But if there is any truth to it I want to hear it and I want to hear it from your lips. So let me ask you again: With-in the last week or week and a half, have you been smoking dope with any of the guys on your floor? (19)

CARL: Uh, well, yeah, but, you know, like it was really discreet. You know, like Sam, he's, man he's smoking dope in the hall half the time, door wide open and all that kind of stuff, and uh, I mean, I come down on him when I see it. And you know, we have a good staff here. You told me last week I was one of your best R.A.s—one of the best R.A.s you've ever had around this place. (20)

STEVE: You are. Right. (21)

CARL: And I do my job, so, like we were just up there and it was one o'clock in the morning and everybody else was in bed, we didn't have the stereo up loud, we had a wet towel under the door, and it wasn't like we called the Army/Navy Band to let everybody know what was going on. It was real discreet. (22)

STEVE: Okay, so maybe it seems a little bit unfair that Sam can walk down the hall smoking dope and then we write a policy about him, but here I am getting on your case and you're discreet about it and it doesn't bother anybody. (23)

CARL: Well, sure! Yeah! (24)

STEVE: Well, you see I still have a problem with that, Carl. Because there's an inconsistency going on here. Now as for Sam, you're right in writing him up if you catch him doing that, but you know, you're also right in that you have to maintain consistency between what you took on as responsibilities as an R.A. and your lifestyle. (25)

CARL: Yeah, but you see consistency depends upon whether or not the policies that you are supposed to uphold are even valid. I mean, this stupid dope policy—I mean, tell the administration to blow it out the ear 'cause it stinks, man. I mean, like second floor. They've been drugging themselves up with alcohol every other night for the last month, you know, and nothing happens there. I mean, they're wasting their brains and here I am, I get together twice in the last year, in the last four months so far, with two of my buddies, just three of us, and I mean this is the whole second floor wiping themselves out. (26)

STEVE: Right. If I were saying this because it was a question of whether people were hurting themselves or not then it wouldn't hold water. I'm not comparing you to second floor, Carl, and you are one of my best R.A.s! I want to let you know that again. I've respected the work you've done in the last year. You've done a super job. And one of the reasons I've respected you is because you've done such a good job on maintaining consistency in your own life as well as in the lives of the guys on the floor. You remember when guys busted the window down there last semester, you went and talked to them, you explained to them all the ramifications of that, but you still had to report them. Carl, I'm in the same position. You are doing something that is inconsistent with the job responsibilities that you took on. Now let's just go over those for a minute. Do you realize that when you took on the job as R.A., that when you did that you also made the pledge to uphold the campus rules and regulations, no matter how bogus they may appear to be? Do you realize that? (27)

CARL: Yeah. But, I mean, it's another thing to say I'm going to do that and to really live it out. (28)

STEVE: That's exactly what it is. You're right. It is another thing. But the campus and I expect that as an R.A. that you will indeed live out what you pledged yourself to do. Is there any reason that I should accept or expect anything less from you? Should I expect inconsistency from one of my best R.A.s? (29)

CARL: I guess I'm still not clear why it's inconsistent, Steve, if I don't believe it's a good rule. (30)

STEVE: Okay. We aren't talking about the validity of the rule. Maybe that's what I should boil it down to. We're talking about you being an R.A. and as a result of being an R.A. your taking upon yourself the desire and the willingness to follow campus rules. You took that on when you became an R.A. No one forced you to become an R.A. No one held a gun to your back. I didn't force you to do it, and, boy, I'm glad you're an R.A. and I don't want to lose you as one. But, Carl, right now you're living in a contradiction of that pledge that you took, and that contradiction is enough to cost you your job. (31)

CARL: I mean this is really bizarre. You know? Cause I'm doing a good job all year long and then I just came down here to tell you that I just saved you a half-hour of time. I was upstairs knee-deep in muck in the bathroom trying to fix the stupid toilet and I come down here and you tell me my job's on the line. (32)

STEVE: Boy, I really appreciate the work you do! And Carl, you're my best one! You're my best R.A.! That's why it hurts me so much and disappoints me so much when I see you living one thing and yet having claimed to do another. That's inconsistent and that's hypocritical, and I know in our talks that we've had together you don't like hypocrisy, you don't like inconsistency, you've told me that before. So doesn't it seem just a little odd that you, then, would live inconsistently whether you think the rule is bad or not? Wouldn't you agree with me that you are living inconsistently between the pledge that you made as an R.A. and actually what you're doing with regards to dope on your floor? (33)

CARL: Well, yeah. I mean there's not much I can say there. (34)

STEVE: Okay. I appreciate your honesty, okay, and I realize that that's frustrating for you because here's a rule that you don't think is legitimate and [is] not valid, and yet at the same time you are forced to maintain it. At the same time, that's exactly what I and the school expect you to do. (35)

CARL: Yeah. (36)

STEVE: Now, let me simply explain something to you, okay? If the rule is bogus and if you really dislike it, there is something you can do. You can go through the proper channels, and you and I can spend some time tomorrow if you want to talk about that, the proper channels as to how you can go about calling that policy into question. But that doesn't allow you the possibility though, to continue being inconsistent with regards to the policy. In other words, what I'm saying, Carl, is that your job is at stake, in a nutshell. I don't want to lose you. We're good friends, you're a good R.A., but Carl, I'll have to take this to the higher-ups if you don't stop. I don't want to, but my job requires me to. Do you understand that? (37)

CARL: Yeah. I mean, I want you to understand, I think we're friends, and uh . . . (38)

STEVE: We are. (39)

CARL: I guess I'm a reasonable enough guy to know that you're telling me this isn't the basis of our friendship. (40)

STEVE: Oh, right. Right. (41)

CARL: I'm really P.O.'d but, uh, you're right, I mean, I was smoking dope. (42)

STEVE: I can understand why you're P.O.'d. You came down here to hand me this report and I lay a bomb on you, I know that. But the reason I'm doing it is because I really like you. I like the job you've done. I like you as a friend. So as a friend I'm going to be up-front with you. And to be up front with you, let me point it out again. Your job is in jeopardy, if you don't begin right now living up to the regulations of the school with regards to dope policy. In other words, that means that you start today, no more smoking dope on your floor. No more smoking dope in this building. I can't stop you from smoking dope if you do it somewhere else, but in this building, which is under my jurisdiction, no more. Now this is what I have to ask you. I need a "yes" or a "no" from you as to whether you're going to pledge yourself to be consistent with the policy or not. (43)

CARL: Well, yeah, I can say that now but when I go upstairs, okay, I gotta tell Pete and I gotta tell Larry, "I can't smoke dope with you guys any more." And those guys, one, they're going to laugh in my face and, two, when I say I can't smoke dope any more they're going to go ahead and do it anyway and then when I catch . . . maybe I'll catch them doing it. What am I supposed to do? They're two of my best friends and I write those guys up, oh, man. . . . (44)

STEVE: Okay. (45)

CARL: . . . they're going to torch my door, they're going to—that's the end of my friendship with those guys. (46)

STEVE: Okay. You're in a bind there, and that's a lot of pressure. I can understand that. The first place we have to start, though, is with your lifestyle. Now that's our first step. And I need to get from you that pledge. If I get the pledge that you're saying "yes, I'll be consistent with the policy, I won't smoke any more dope on my floor," then you and I can sit down and talk about how we're going to go about dealing with those two guys. I don't want you to lose your friendship with them. And I can help you in any way possible to help you do this. (47)

CARL: Okay, I'll make you a deal then. (48)

STEVE: All right. (49)

CARL: We'll do that. I mean, I'll do it. I'll quit. (50)

STEVE: You'll do what? (51)

CARL: I'll quit smoking dope. (52)

STEVE: Okay. (53)

CARL: If you and I get together tomorrow night like, maybe for dinner or something, and we hash this through because I, I don't know, I mean I'm uh, if I don't, if you know . . . I like doing this job, I like you, but, and if I lose this job I lose eight hundred dollars financial support, I'm gone, I'll never see you again. I'll never see this school again. So, uh, I mean I need to work this through with you. (54)

STEVE: I'd really like to do that. Okay? Having you as an R.A. and as a friend, I want to do that. So let's you and I get together tomorrow night for dinner and we'll talk about the ramifications of this with regards to those guys on your floor and maybe any other things. We can just talk about that, and also, maybe, if you want, to we can talk about how you go about changing policy in regard to that rule. Okay? (55)

CARL: Okay. (56)

STEVE: But are we understood, from this point on, I will have no reason to expect any more reports that you've been smoking dope with people, not because people haven't caught you, but because you are not going to smoke any more dope in this building. Do I have that pledge from you? (57)

CARL: Yeah, you got it. (They shake hands.) (58)

STEVE: Thanks, friend. Thanks a lot. See you tomorrow for dinner. (59)

CARL: Good. All right. Bye-bye. (60)

STEVE: Goodbye.

First Critique

What's your general impression? Do you like Steve's style? Many people have appreciated his blend of "gentle" and "tough." I recall well a session on human-relations skills I taught for production supervisors in a large cookie bakery. After listening to this twice on a tape, one of the participants, a man with twenty-five years service as a foreman on the production line, said, "I'd love to work for a guy like that."

I saw tears in the man's eyes, which I believe were from his genuine longing to work for someone who would hold him to a high standard of accountability for his actions, and at the same time would care deeply about his personal welfare. That is rare. Steve accomplishes both in this conversation.

You can learn to do it just as well. To improve your own understanding and skills, please read the script again. This time give more attention to the specific communication vehicles used. Notice how often Steve praises Carl for the many things Carl has been doing well in his job. It will be helpful to mark the various kinds of communication: M for mirroring, I for I-statements, C for confrontation, U for ultimatums, and P for praise. This will help you see how "gentle" and "tough" styles blend together for an effect that is forceful without antagonizing the other person. When you've read it a second time, skip this critique and go directly to the second critique, below.

Second Critique

Now let's look at the script in more detail. As you go through the numbered commentary below, please go back to the corresponding part of the script to review its context.

20. When Carl says "it was really discreet," Steve does not pounce on him. Steve is quite patient in this interview—energetic, but patient.

21. Steve affirms what he can about Carl's job performance.

23. Steve shows he understands that Carl feels he is being treated unfairly.

25. "I still have a problem with that" is an "I-message." "You're right in writing him up" affirms Carl's action. "You're also right . . ." begins to confront.

27. This section contains a lot of affirmation. By making the affirmation more concrete with the broken-window example it is more powerful. Then Steve makes the infraction equally concrete by saying, "Do you realize that when you took. . . ."

29. "You're right" is affirmation. Steve agrees when he can, which makes it easier for Carl to accept Steve's disagreements later. "It is another thing . . ." is mirroring of the content.

31. "I'm glad you're an R.A." is an affirmation. But note that right on the heels of that is the ultimatum, ". . . that contradiction is enough to cost you your job."

33. More affirmation. Then, in the middle of that a confrontation with Carl's own stated beliefs, ". . . you don't like hypocrisy . . . you've told me that before." Carl's own words confront him with power that Steve's words don't have.

35. Mirroring.

37. Steve gives all the options and leaves it as Carl's choice. He closes with a restatement of the previous ultimatum, and shows willingness to help in a concrete way.

43. "You're P.O.'d . . . I lay a bomb on you," is mirroring. "I really like you" and the following words are affirmation. Steve then restates the ultimatum, "Your job is in jeopardy . . ." and makes a clear summary of the expectations and closes by asking for a concrete response. Throughout, Steve's caring and concern for Carl's welfare, as well as the gravity of the matter, come through Steve's tone of voice as well as through his words.

47. This statement begins with mirroring, repeats the demand, and shows Steve's caring through his offer to help in any way possible.

51. Persistence.
55. Again Steve shows warmth.
57. Steve repeats his expectation.

Summary

The most important element in this dialogue does not show up in specific words, but is intermingled throughout. That is Steve's honest concern for Carl's best interests. Steve is looking out for himself, sure. He has a job to do.

But Carl also has a job to do, and Steve is determined that Carl not be hurt by his (Carl's) failure to do that job well. Steve is not willing for Carl to live with less than complete job performance, or with less than complete personal integrity, based on Carl's own standards.

Because Steve cares, he does not rest until he has Carl's commitment to do the job the way he must. And because Steve cares, he uses communication styles that reject Carl's behavior without rejecting Carl. It's beautifully done.

And *you* can put it all together as well as Steve did.

PART TWO

How to Fix
Hard Situations
the Easy Way

7

How to Say No

"Oh, if I'd only said no!"

"I just couldn't bring myself to say no."

"Whenever someone wants me to do something, I do it. It's easier to go along than to say no, because saying no makes me feel guilty."

How many times have we heard someone say things like these? And, sometimes, the person is you or me!

The Basis for Saying No

You have a *right* to say no to requests that are unreasonable or do not interest you. You are entitled, thanks to the freedoms of our country, to pick and choose. Whoopee!

You are *responsible* to say no to requests that would be hurtful to other persons. This responsibility rests on all of us. We take this on if we want to help create a world that is good to live in. This includes saying no to requests that would hurt the person who makes the request. If we don't, we enable that person's self-destruction.

We ought to say no to requests that are immoral or illegal for the same reason. And it's right and proper to say no to those requests that would overtax our ability to do the things that are more important.

The Obstacles

Saying no is often difficult because it sets up the possibility of rejection. Most of us are interested in pleasing people; we don't like rejection. That's an obstacle.

But not to say no when you should is a quick trip into the dumpster. When you say yes to someone else's request, it often means saying no to one of your own needs or desires. A little of that is healthy, but too much of it is personal disaster. To overcome this obstacle, the fear of their rejection, refuse to reject *yourself*.

The other person's insistence is another obstacle. Overcome this obstacle with the communication vehicles in this chapter.

The Map

Learn to say no.

It's a simple word. Using it is not all negative. In fact, one of the worst things a person can do in a friendship is never to say no. Never saying no encourages and allows others to make demands you can't fulfill, with the result that you get overly busy and stressed out. Sooner or later your anger will reach the point that you get back at your friend—bad stuff for both of you.

So saying no is a valuable part of friendship and is necessary to keep your own life in order.

If it has been hard for you to say no, it can become easy. The first three sections of the trip are especially easy:

1. *Get more information.* Before you make a decision, be sure you are clear about what the other person wants. If you're not clear, *ask!* You owe it to both of you to know what is going on before you decide. There is nothing risky or difficult about asking people to tell you more about what they want: That's what they want to talk about. You can even ask for more information as a way of giving yourself more time to think about the request.

2. *Listen well before you decide.* Your listening shows respect; it is a compliment to the speaker. What's not to like about that? Pretty easy!

3. *Postpone the decision.* It's a lot better to delay a decision than to make a bad decision. Better for both of you. Say, "This is important to you. It is to me, too. For that reason, I need to think it over." Give things a chance to settle down. This is reasonable. If the other person wants to push you into a quick decision, beware. That's probably a sure sign you will be better off saying no.

4. *Say no.* If you're going to decline, the best way to do it is with the plain and simple little word, *no.* To get results, use it. Say "no." We'll see some variations below, but they each must include clearly the word *no.*

5. *Listen after you've said no.* Let the other person talk about anything he or she wants want to, including anger toward you for saying no, if that's the case. Your listening is an act of great respect toward the other person. If he or she is angry, it's better for both of you that the anger is vented now so you can be done with it than to let it smolder. If he or she gives you more sales pitch for the request, you might listen to that briefly without comment.

6. *Stick to your decision.* You've made the best decision you could. Don't second-guess yourself unnecessarily.

In general, saying no successfully is usually a combination of:

- Being warm and polite—*yet* firmly refusing
- Being patient and deliberate—*yet* decisive
- Thinking, *You're okay,*—but *your request isn't*
- Expressing "I'm interested in you,"—*but* "I'm not interested in your request"
- Showing empathy for the other person—*with* protection for yourself
- Considering your options—*and sticking with your choice*

The Vehicle

Again, we travel around the obstacle in the vehicles of technique. In this discussion, the technique is communication. Both the words and their nonverbal style of delivery are important.

When saying no, be clear. If you are vague, it encourages the other person to keep pushing on you. Be brief, yet complete.

There are several styles to choose from, though you may not need to use more than one. These are listed in order of increasing "toughness," but you do not need to use them in this sequence. You may use the same style several times in a row. You'll use your own judgment in the situation you are in.

1. *A simple no.* The slogan, "Just say no" has been widely advertised. It's advice that works. Just say "no"—or "no, thank you." That's all.

2. *An empathic no.* Along with saying no, show interest in the other person's feelings about the request, or his or her feelings about being turned down. Use the skill of mirroring from chapter 2. Expressing empathy (by mirroring), shows you have accurately heard the other person. It softens the rejection carried by the no because it proves that you care about him or her as a person, even though you are rejecting the request.

3. *No with a reason.* This is a style you may use frequently. Explain, simply and quickly, why you say no. Be brief! The

more you say, the more likely you are to encourage the other person to keep trying to talk you into changing your mind. Do not debate the merits of your reasons. That only encourages the person to keep pestering you.

4. *No with an alternative.* You might just suggest alternatives, or you might offer to help out in some way other than doing what the person asked for. In doing this, do not take over the responsibility for solving the problem unless you are willing to help out that much, and unless doing so is in the other person's best interests. Otherwise you are encouraging him or her to become dependent on you.

5. *No with an I-statement.* Using this technique, you say no—but also report the effect the other person's pushiness is having on you.

6. *The broken-record method.* This simply means that you keep repeating your "no" response over and over and over again, clearly and politely each time, until the message gets across.

You wish to reject the request without appearing to reject the "requester" as a person. You wouldn't want to say one thing with your words and another through your nonverbal style. It's easy to do both well. As to the nonverbal, it's mostly a matter of *not* doing things. Don't smile, at least not much. Don't growl. And so on. Your style should be quite neutral. Here are some guidelines:

Facial expression:	Not smiling; face matches the seriousness of your words
Eye contact:	Steady
Body position:	Face directly at same level or a little above
Body movement:	Relaxed; moving away
Energy level:	Restrained but forceful (power under control)
Loudness of voice:	Avoid soft voice; loudness up to matching their loudness. Talking too

	loudly will sound like rejection of the other person.
Tone of voice:	Firm and businesslike
Flow of words:	Smooth continuity of thoughts; precise and distinct
Pitch Level:	Low pitch is usually interpreted as confidence. Talk in your "airline pilot's voice."

The Best Shortcut

Your vehicle of "no" will be more attractive to others if you coat it with empathy—genuine interest in their concerns. This does not mean you *agree* with their view, only that you *understand* it. Mirroring helps you have and communicate empathy.

Wrong Turns

You're headed for an accident if your nonverbal style is gruff or abrupt. Your greatest hazard is in getting worn down by the other person's continuing begging. Shut that off. Change the subject or leave if you must. If you give in, you teach the person to "get over" on you. Giving in is like wearing a sign on your back that says, "I'm a sucker." Don't.

Examples of the Easy Way

Let's put this together and see how it might work. A neighbor you don't know well is speaking to you. She says, "I have the most wonderful news! I'm going on vacation to Las Vegas! I have free transportation there and back with a woman from work. All I have to pay is food and my share of the room rent, which won't be much. I have enough money for that, but, uh, unfortunately, I don't have any, uh, shall we say, spending money. You know, for the games and like that. Will you loan me five hundred dollars? I'll pay it back as soon as I get back, and give you a hundred extra out of my winnings."

Now, you might want to shove half a grapefruit in the neighbor's face, along with a few insults, but let's be civilized instead. It's easier. Here are some possible responses:

1. *A simple no.* "No." It doesn't get any simpler than that. You can't beat it for being clear and convenient. It works.

2. *An empathic no.* "Well, you're sure excited about that! It's obvious that you are looking forward to it, but, no, that's not something I can help you with." See the mirroring of feelings—"you're sure excited" and "you are looking forward to it." Recall from chapter 2 that mirroring the other person's feelings can bring some powerful benefits. You'll get a hunk of those same benefits here—a good effect to mix in with the disappointment from the no. It helps soften the sting. Or you could say, "I guess it's disappointing for you that I'm saying no, but that's my answer." This time the negative feelings are bounced back by the mirroring. That's good, too, because it shows that you care enough to listen.

3. *No with a reason.* "No. I don't have that kind of money available," or "No. Using money that way, especially when it's necessary to borrow it, doesn't seem to me to be in your best interests. For that reason, I wouldn't be comfortable supporting your venture." Or you might say, "No, basically because gambling is an industry I don't wish to be part of, even indirectly. This is a personal belief and maybe you don't agree, and it's okay if you don't, but that's one of the reasons why I am saying no to your request." Just offer the reason; don't get in a debate explaining it. Defending it is a dead-end street. Don't go there; just give the reason and let it go.

4. *No with an alternative.* "No. Count me out of that. But, what other plans have you thought of?" or "No. Have you thought of other sources, such as getting cash through your Visa card?" or "No. You see, the travel part of it sounds okay to me, but the other part doesn't. If there are ways I can help you with something else, I could consider that, but not this." Warning: In the

same way that arguing about your reasons for saying no is a dead-end street, offering an alternative may also lead you into a trap. Be cautious. It's not your job to find a solution to the other person's problem. But if you really want to, and can avoid getting cornered into doing his or her work, make some suggestions.

5. *No with an I-statement.* "No. This is the third time you have asked me that this morning. My answer is the same, and it will continue to be no if you continue to ask me. I hope that you won't keep asking me because it is getting to be a nuisance. I will talk about something else. For example: How will you go there?" Or you could say, "No. You continue to ask and, frankly, the repeated asking is becoming a bother to me. My answer is no. I've tried to make that clear, and to help you understand my point of view. I hope you will not ask again about that, because I am unwilling to do it or to talk about doing it. If you ask me again, it will only annoy me." The I-statement, a basic skill from chapter 3, helps you talk about what you need. It's handy here to cut off the conversation. Note that the second example is more intense than the first.

Summary

No matter how unappealing it might be to say no in some situations, if you need to say no it will be much easier in the long run if you say it rather than not say it. Hasn't that been your experience?

So here's hoping that everything that comes your way is something you can say yes to. But since you and I both know that will not be the case, do the next best thing. Say no when you need to. Avoid the hassles that come from caving in to outside pressure. Just say no.

PERSONAL ACTION PLAN

Situation:
(Person) _____
wants me to _____

Obstacle: (Check) ___ My fear of rejection
                       ___ Other person's persistence
                       ___ Other: _____

Vehicle:
Reasons to say no: _____
My feelings: _____
I-statement: _____

Shortcut:
I'll use mirroring to understand the other person better
and show that I care. I suspect his or her feelings might be
_____.
Using mirroring, I might say:
You feel _____
because _____.

Contract with myself:
I will say no. I will do so because it is best for me.
Although it may be inconvenient and/or disappointing to
_____ , it is not detrimental to him or her.

Yes, I'll say "no!"

(signed) _____

(date)   _____

8

How to Say the
Right Thing
When There's
Nothing to Say

Harry described being unable to awaken his wife and discovering that she had deliberately overdosed. With sobs and in broken words he told about sitting in a chair beside her hospital bed for three days and nights not knowing if she would live. Then he asked, "Can you imagine what that was like?"

During a coffee break at a seminar, Ingrid told me that within the last eight months her father had died, her mother had died, and her husband had died. Then she waited for me to speak.

With a snarl and a sneer, Jack, a heroin addict, challenged, "What makes you think you know anything about what life in hell has been like for me?"

The Obstacle

Events far beyond our own experience may shock or confuse us to the point that we are speechless. We may want to say something but be afraid that we will say the wrong thing and hurt the other person. We worry about appearing foolish. So we mumble, fumble, and sweat, and later we explain weakly to a friend, "There was nothing to say."

We all know how difficult these situations can be. No one thinks less of us if we're awkward at these times. But we would be more comfortable if we were sure we could handle those situations in which there is nothing to say.

Wrong Turns

In truth, there were many things that could have been said. Some would have been insulting. "Harry, her life with you must have been pretty miserable if she wanted to end it that way."

Other comments might turn defensive. We wish to hide our insecurity behind "de" fence. We may try to bluff our way out of it, saying, "Hey, Jack, you can't tell me anything I don't already know about."

Other comments are air-headed or at best, meaningless. We babble to cover our uneasiness.

What's Wrong with This Conversation?

The setting: Visitation at the funeral home at the time of my father's death. A visitor gushed to me, "I know just how you feel. I have lost my father, too."

Maybe nothing's wrong with it, but I'll tell you what I thought just after I heard it: *Okay, I guess you've known some real sorrow. But you don't know how I feel because you only lost an ordinary father. At most you lost a great father, but I have lost the most wonderful father in the world. So you don't know how I feel.*

I knew the person had tried. The effort meant something, but those words didn't.

But I Loved These Folks . . .

Among those who came through the visitation line were some who didn't try to say much of anything. They let their grief show in their eyes and they let their caring flow from the warmth of a slow, gentle handclasp.

Tears came to their eyes because they had been through similar pain, but they did not talk of that; when they spoke it was of my loss, not theirs—my grief, not theirs. The tears were for my pain, not theirs. Though they were strangers to me, I was nourished and I loved them for it.

The first step in saying the right thing in difficult situations is to not say the wrong thing. To avoid that, *listen.*

A Universal Desire

The Old Testament character, Job, is described as "the greatest man among all the people of the East" (Job 1:3). He had incredible wealth until a day of great calamity. It is written that on that one day his five hundred oxen and five hundred donkeys were stolen by one group and his three thousand camels were stolen by a different group. His seven thousand sheep were burned up by fire that fell from the sky, a large number of servants were murdered, and his seven sons and three daughters were killed when a violent windstorm destroyed their house (1:13–19).

In the aftermath of this devastation, Job wanted to be heard. At one point he begged his friends to listen. Job says "listen to the plea of my lips" (13:6), "keep silent and let me speak" (13:13), and "listen carefully to my words" (13:17). When his friend Eliphaz gives a speech, Job retorts, "Will your long-winded speeches never end? What ails you that you keep on arguing?" (Job 16:3).

You or I might have shouted, "Shut up and listen, will ya?"

When Job was in pain, he didn't want to hear a speech. Job wanted his friend to give him the gift of listening. It is a universal desire.

I would like for you to be better in your friendships than Job's friends were to him. I would like for you to be the type of person Job needed. That type of relationship begins by recognizing what the other person is seeking from you. Your response can then be guided by what that person needs, not by what is convenient for you. In doing so, you will respond as Job would have liked when he pled to his friend, "listen carefully to my words."

Give Yourself a Break

In these "nothing-to-say" situations, fewer words usually create more communication. Instead of babbling, listen. Instead of fumbling for brilliance and mumbling a cliché, listen. Instead of worrying about you, think about them—listen.

If, while listening, you avoid a wrong turn, congratulate yourself. The beginning of sensitivity is the reduction of clumsiness. From now on, take note of blunders you don't make and give yourself credit for safe driving during those near misses.

A Map

Now, I'll offer a plan to follow in situations when there is nothing to say: Unless you know positively what to say, put all your attention upon the situation of the other person. Let him or her take the conversation wherever he or she would like it to go. You follow that lead.

Use the method of mirroring because it lets you learn from the other person, who is, after all, the world's authority on himself or herself. People in sad or stressful situations may not see themselves accurately or completely, but they have spent more time with themselves than anyone else has. They've been there. (Why is it so easy for us to ignore that and act as though we know more about them than they do?)

Listen. Learn about them. Then, you'll know what else to do. If it would be better to confront, give advice, or use some other method, you will. Whatever may come up, you can handle by selecting the most useful map and vehicle.

But first, listen. By that, and only by that, can you know what to say.

A Vehicle

When you don't know what to say, use the technique of mirroring you learned in chapter 2. It is a useful vehicle in the situations described in this chapter. For example, let's go back to the funeral home visitation scene just mentioned.[1]

I recall other things that were said that meant a lot to me then (and, sixteen years later, still mean a lot). I picture clearly the faces of people whose words comforted me, even though I had no notion of who they were or what their relationship with my father had been. Many phrases are examples of the technique of mirroring:

"It must be really, really hard." (Books on writing style would give that comment a failing grade; my heart gives it an A+.)

"I imagine it might seem unfair to you that he's gone."

"You probably wonder how long it's going to take to get over it. And you know that, even though in a way you will get over it, life will never be the same."

"It must be harder than any of us can know."

---

1. Is it crass to analyze comments made during visitation at the time of my father's death? No, not crass—convincing. We do not change our behavior until we are emotionally convinced we ought to. It is important to me that you learn the importance of good relationships, and of the power communication has in your relationshps. It is not likely that examples drawn from my life will influence you to change any of your patterns. But as you take examples from your own life, they will convince you. It is my hope that by sharing some of my experiences with you, you will become alert to your own life experiences and learn from them. Life is a classroom that dismisses only at death. Instead of daydreaming about recess, we would be better off to discover that learning is not only more valuable, it is more fun.

Other comments that are memorable because of their benefit are examples of I-statements:

"I don't know what to say. It hurts so much."

"It leaves me numb with sorrow—for my own loss, and for yours."

This one was written: "I looked and looked for a card, but nothing said how I felt. And I can't say it either. So please understand that I would rather send only this little note that doesn't say anything, than say something that is too small." Of all the cards and letters, this meant the most to me.

Now let's see how mirroring and I-statements would work with a different type of situation.

The Case of Surly Jack, the Addict

Jack had just been sent to one of our residences by the welfare board. His face looked as ragged, wrinkled, and grimy as his scruffy clothing. Still in his early twenties, he looked old, unhealthy, and battered—worn out.

JACK: What makes you think you know anything about what life in hell has been like for me? (defiantly) You do-gooders can sit back and think you're hot stuff, but you don't know nothing!

EASY WAY: You've been through a lot, Jack. More than most people could have survived, I guess.

(Comment: Don't pretend. The world may be getting smaller, but the information in it is getting larger. Why should I pretend I know very much at all about anything? I don't.)

JACK: I'm tough.

EASY Way: I hear you. Tough enough to survive a hell on earth.

JACK: You wouldn't know about that.

EASY WAY: Our lives have been different; you're right about that. It sounds like your life has been an ordeal, but you've been strong enough to make it.

JACK: I'm tough.

EASY WAY: You feel good about that.

(Comment: I'm not endorsing his brand of toughness, just showing that I recognize how he regards it. At the same time, I can give genuine respect for his capacity for survival.[2])

JACK: Sure, 'cause I wouldn't have made it any other way. If you ain't tough, you ain't worth anything because you ain't going to make it.

EASY WAY: But you've made it. What you've been through, I don't know, but you've survived. You've gotta be pretty proud of that.

JACK: You're dang right.

(Comment: Again, give him credit for every good thing he's done.)

EASY WAY: Earlier you said I don't know what life has been like for you. You're right about that—I don't. But I'd like to, if you'd like to help me with that. Want to tell me some more about your life and help me understand it as best I can?

(Comment: An invitation for more conversation, not a demand.)

JACK: Maybe another time.

EASY WAY: Yeah, that'd be good. Maybe tomorrow.

JACK: Yeah, tomorrow.

(Comment: Was the conversation successful? I think so, because: (1) the nonverbal signs of his anger settled

2. Addicts do go to hell and back. Well, more go than come back—but those who survive do so because they possess at least a few remarkable personal abilities. Scrape away the slime attitudes and scum behavior and one often finds a person of remarkable talents if those abilities have not been destroyed by the addictive lifestyle.

*down as we talked, and (2) we had a jovial conversa-
tion the next day.)*

Shortcuts

If we think of a technique as a vehicle for communication, a "shortcut" represents the things we might do to get where we want to go more easily and quickly. That is the purpose of the "Shortcuts" sections in this and other chapters.

When people have emotional burdens that can't be fixed, it is still helpful to them to talk about those burdens. Mirroring responses are helpful in these situations because they allow the talkers to release tension and know that even though you, the listener, cannot change the situation, you care enough to listen and to understand as best you can.

When talkers have a problem to solve, they are likely to see the problem more clearly as mirroring continues. Since most people are sensible and try to solve their own problems, they probably will work out some solutions on their own. Mirroring is often much more helpful than giving advice.

The skill of mirroring has another benefit to both persons: when you use the skill of mirroring you are not doing any of the things that can disrupt the relationship. When you're using mirroring you are not giving advice, you are not condemning, you are not getting off the subject that is most important to the talker. Mirroring helps you stay on track and stay out of trouble. These are good benefits. But mirroring is not always the best choice. Don't use the skill of mirroring in these situations:

1. When the other person is seeking information or needs immediate action.

2. When the other person needs to be confronted. The methods in chapter 4 will be more effective, with mirroring interspersed as lubricant.

3. When the other person is not in touch with reality, is suicidal, intoxicated, or depressed.

4. When the other person is trying to manipulate you with anger, use the strategies in chapter 18.

Summary

Mirroring is handy. To some people it has seemed like nonsense at first impression. But it is powerful, especially in situations when there are no pat answers. Try it out. Give people a chance to tell you about themselves. In so doing, you will understand them better and learn more about life. It's also likely that the experience of great acceptance that your mirroring responses provide will be helpful to the other person.

Action Planning

Now it's time for you to drive down the road of your choice. How about a practice spin? You can do that by looking at a "nothing-to-say" situation you have already been through, and then planning and rehearsing a situation that is part of your life now.

The action plans will lead you into the best part of the learning you will get from this book. All the book can do is prepare you to get some education in "real life." It is there that you will discover how to integrate the principles and skills into your own special personal style. I urge you to take seriously the opportunities you have today. Then tomorrow, re-read the chapter, thoughtfully work out an action plan, and put it into practice. Happy learning!

PERSONAL ACTION PLAN

Situation from the past:
(Person) had this going on: _____
His or her content: _____
His or her probable feelings: _____

Mirroring responses I might have given:
"You feel _____
because _____."

I-statements I might have given:
"Knowing that (their content) _____
I feel (your feelings, his or her content) _____
_____."

A present situation:
(Person) has this going on: _____
His or her content: _____
His or her probable feelings: _____

Mirroring responses I might give:
"You feel _____
because _____."

I-statements I might give:
"Knowing that (their content) _____
I feel (your feelings, his or her content) _____
_____."

It will be very helpful to rehearse this with someone before having your next conversation with the hurting person.
Who could role play this with you?
When? Call that person now, set a time, and record it here:

_____

I'll do it!

(signed) _____

(date) _____

9

How to Set Things Right After You've Been Given Bad Service or Defective Merchandise

When a man lost a quarter in the restaurant's jukebox, the waitress told him the cashier would refund it to him. While paying his bill he asked the cashier about it. She said tartly, "We've been having a lot of trouble with those machines. I can't do anything about that. You lost a quarter."

"Then you lost a customer," the man said, calmly enough.

The cashier shrieked, "For a quarter?"

"My thought, *exactly*," the man replied as he left, never to return.

Good service is hard to find.

When I called the police department to tell them that the suspect in the burglary of my house had been seen committing another theft nearby within the last few minutes, the dispatcher seemed disinterested.

"Who are you?" he asked, although I had identified myself. "Are you just a citizen?"

I bellowed. "*Just* a citizen? I thought that was *enough!*"

Good service is hard to find—even harder than finding my burglar.

Conditions force us to learn how to complain. We must master the skills of drawing from people the remedies for bad service or faulty products received from them or their organization.

It's not easy. The modern slogan seems to be, "the customer is always right, but only until we make the sale." Now, due in part to the widespread selfishness of the last couple decades, apathy seems to supplant enthusiasm, indifference supplants concern, politics supplants statesmanship, and competition supplants collaboration. We must be able to complain effectively to survive.

Obstacles

For many people, it's a hassle. They don't want to make waves. They don't want to be rejected. They don't want to held at bay by a clerk or a contractor who may find shouting loud and ugly at them an enjoyable break in an otherwise uneventful day. Some people need to overcome the obstacle of their own fear.

Dealing with these situations may be emotional for other reasons. Perhaps there is fear that we have made a bad decision: buyer's remorse. We spent money on something we couldn't afford, and now it's not working. There may be grief over the shattered dream. A recent TV report chronicled the financial nightmare of a family that paid twenty thousand dollars for an in-ground swimming pool that was incorrectly built by a company that went bankrupt. There went the happy summer for those folks. Getting things corrected may call for us to be in a conflict scenario while we are emotionally as drained as that broken swimming pool.

Another obstacle is difficulty in finding the right person to file your complaint with. Even when phoning for telephone repair a few days ago I was transferred five times (and I think the phone companies work very hard, and very well, at customer relations). But life today is complex. My phone book has thirty-two pages of instructions at the front, approximately the size of the entire phone book for the little town where I grew up.

Given our emotional state and the difficulty of the task, there are plenty of chances to take a wrong turn. Let's look at three of the more common ones.

Wrong Turns

While writing this chapter I chatted with a friend who has twenty years experience as an automotive service department manager. We talked about different approaches people take in complaining about bad service. I asked him about the effectiveness of tantrums as a way of obtaining better service. He just laughed. Wow, did he laugh!

In most places, especially with low-echelon employees, belligerence is much more likely to be damaging than to be beneficial.

Rudeness, cheap threats, tantrums, name calling, and other personal attacks have no place on your list of strategies. There may be a place for the threat of legal action or filing a complaint with an agency, but do that only after you have exhausted other means, and do it in a well-reasoned, polite fashion.

Another wrong turn is to be half-hearted. Don't say anything like, "I don't suppose you would. . . ." or "I'm sure you can't help, but. . . ." These openings invite the person to say no before he or she even hears your complaint.

Nor should you beg. This shows weakness when you need to be showing strength.

A third wrong turn is to give up too quickly. This is a short dead-end street. Persist. Take the process step by step. Success for the day is to have done all that you can do in that day to move toward solving the problem. The action plan will help you keep track of your progress.

A Map

Here is the trip to take: Organize the facts about your problem, decide what action you want, find the person who can provide it, then clearly ask for what you want. To be persuasive, you need to be able to tell the person the consequences he or she will experience if you don't get what you want. Let's go over these elements one by one.

1. *Organize the facts.* Set up a file or envelope where you can keep track of everything. Write down the facts—date, cost, who you talked with, location, and so on. What are you complaining about? When was service requested? Even though this information is fresh in your mind now, as you proceed with the process it will be handy to have it written down in one place. Find your receipt and any other papers associated with the transaction, including any warranty information that came from the manufacturer.

2. *Define what you want.* What are you going to ask for? Do you prefer a refund? Repair? Exchange? Credit toward something else?

3. *Find the right person to deal with.* Don't deal with the computer, find a person! Any time you talk with someone, by phone or in person, get that person's name and put it in your notes. If that person cannot give you satisfaction, ask for the name of his or her supervisor.

While it is essential for you to have a contact person within the organization you're dealing with, there are outside resources available to help you. Ask your local Better Business Bureau. Many newspapers and TV stations have trouble-shooting features to help consumers.

Try to find a government body that regulates the business. A booklet, *Consumer's Resource Handbook,* is available free from the Consumer Information Center, Dept. 568X, P. O. Box 100,

Pueblo, CO 81002. This is also available in most libraries, where you will find other resource books that will help you locate regulatory agencies. Libraries are usually aware of agencies interested in consumer protection and advocacy.

4. *Communicate clearly.* If you have a choice of communicating in person or over the phone, decide which is better for you. If you are more comfortable and self-assured over the telephone, that's fine. Either way it is better to avoid complaining the first thing Monday morning or on Friday afternoon. People are more likely to cooperate during the middle of the week.

Do not show signs of weakness or indecision. Be courteous but tough. If you're meeting in person, notice the body language of the other person. Someone who stands erect with no-nonsense mannerisms may respond with less resistance to a soft-sell approach. A person slumped over in lifeless fashion may be used to taking orders and may not offer much resistance.

A person who doesn't make eye contact with you will probably give in rather quickly to your polite pressure. Someone who looks you in the eye but ends contact before you do likely feels weaker than you do and will be responsive to your forceful approach.

If you communicate by letter, keep it short and to the point. Use one paragraph to describe the facts, a second to describe what you are asking for. If this is the first stage in your complaint process, that is probably enough. If, however, your letter follows conversations with other staff people, it is time to show more force. Add a paragraph to describe the actions you will take if the business does not comply with your request.

Type the letter if at all possible. Use good stationery. Be polite; insulting letters are easy to ignore. Check your spelling and grammar carefully. Include all the pertinent facts. Send copies—never originals—of canceled checks, bills, or other documents.

If you have located a person by phone, send it directly to that person. Use certified mail to make sure it gets there. At this time, or later, you may want to write the vice-president of marketing, or even the company president. These names are usually available in reference books such as *Standard and Poor's,* found at the local library.

A strong closing recommended by a business-letter consultant is, "Please give your immediate attention to this important matter or it will be assumed that you do not wish to fulfill your obligation."

You will need to describe the consequences if the other person or business doesn't cooperate. Don't make threats you cannot or will not carry out. For example, it's pointless to say to a salesperson, "I'm going to see that you get fired" or "That remark is going to cost you your job!" Such arrogance will get you nothing other than more resistance.

Vehicles of Communication When Complaining

We find that our faithful communication companions once again rise to the occasion. See how they work in these situations.

Mirroring and Compliments

When at a service counter—the post office, airline check-in, or such place—I don't mind in the least to be the next person served after a belligerent person. In fact, I kind of like it. Hey, it's easier to look like a rose if you stand in the weeds.

I start by mirroring what I believe are the clerk's content and feelings, and add a compliment. For example, "It must be awfully difficult to be as polite as you were to someone as unreasonable as he was. I don't know how you do it." Or I might say, "It must be hard to manage yourself well in all the situations you have here. I heard how you handled that, and I was really impressed with how you kept your cool." Or I simply say, "You're doing a good job."

The next time you get to step up to a counter after someone who was throwing a tantrum, try it and see if you don't get good results, too. Nine out of ten times this approach will put that frazzled clerk in the palm of your hand. For that person it's a glass of cool water after a trip through the furnace, so it usually works, and works beautifully. Remember, though, your interest must be honest.

I once stood in line at the repair counter of a ski shop behind an explosive man who was angrily ranting his demands upon an elderly clerk who seemed, to those of us waiting in line, to be patient and reasonable. The belligerent man identified himself by name, rank, and serial number—a Dr. Blah Blah Blah, chairman of XYZ Department at Such-and-Such University. Now, I ask, what does his academic position have to do with getting served at the ski shop? But three times Dr. BBB from XYZ at SAS U identified himself and his exalted position, as though the clerk should suddenly realize that he was in the presence of greatness and throw the store at the man's angrily fidgeting feet.

When dealing with someone who controls what you want, you'll do a lot better by showing interest in him or her than you will by flaunting credentials that are irrelevant in the situation (no matter how impressive they may be in other circles) or in any other way putting yourself ahead of the other person. *If you would have people understand where you are, first go where they are—which is what I tried to do when it was my turn.*

I said, "I admire the way you conducted yourself while he was throwing all that at you. It must have been hard to take, but you handled it." Bingo! He was happy and gave me good service. I was happy. The people in line behind me, making jokes about the professor, were happy. The livid professor stomped back to his car without getting what he had come for, and the snow melted wherever he stepped.

I-Statements

Just as mirroring comes in handy in other circumstances, I-statements will work well in the following situations, especially in the earlier stages. Here are a few examples:

"I bought this framastan here yesterday, but was quite disappointed to find that it will not rotate as advertised."

"I've been pleased with my experience here many times before, but something that happened today disturbs me, and I think you need to know about it."

"The package doesn't say that your flea powder is highly explosive, so you can imagine how surprised I was when my cat walked close to the fireplace and. . . ."

By now, you know how it works: The I-statement reports feelings about an event. It can also be used to make a request such as, "I would be satisfied if your company would. . . ." or, "I will enjoy shopping at your store again when. . . ."

Questions and Requests

When you are searching for the person who is able to help you, ask, ask, ask. Politely.

"I don't want to bother you needlessly. Is this something you can help me with?"

"Are you empowered to make a decision about this?"

"Is it part of your job to help me resolve this problem?"

"Who *can* help me with this?"

"What is your name?"

"Please transfer me to the person who can help me with this."

Ask. You won't receive without it.

Confrontation

Turn up the pressure. Lay your demands out very clearly:
1. This is the problem.
2. This is the correction I want.
3. When are you going to take care of it?
4. This is what will happen if you don't.

EASY WAY: The framastan moves side to side, but, as your ad states it is also supposed to rotate. It doesn't rotate. I wish to exchange this one for one that will rotate. Are you the person who can take care of this for me?

CLERK: Uh, well, I never seen a—what is it, a frabaslam?— like this here one before.

EASY WAY: Perhaps I should talk with the department manager about this. Who is the manager?

(Comment: Go after it!)

CLERK: Uh, that'd be Mr. Gavin Browning.

EASY WAY: Would you get him for me, please?

   (Comment: Stay after it!)

CLERK: He doesn't work on Saturday.

EASY WAY: Today is Friday.

   (Comment: Hang in there, you're learning patience.)

CLERK: Uh, I'll go look for him.

MR. BROWNING: Hello.

EASY WAY: (repeats request for an exchange)

MR. BROWNING: Sure.

Shortcut

To make it easier for the other parties to cooperate with you, present your information to them in well organized style. Instead of just referring to an earlier letter, send a copy of it. Use their invoice or other reference numbers in your correspondence. When phoning, have all the information at hand so you can give it quickly. Take as much nuisance out of the investigation as you can, so their chore is not with getting the facts, but with getting you satisfied.

Summary

Life is stressful for most people; they're sunburned. Touch them with salve, not sandpaper, and they will (most of them) cooperate wonderfully (most of the time). But carry a toolbox of techniques to use on those who require it.

PERSONAL ACTION PLAN

1. Organize the facts. I am complaining about (item):

_____

_____

This was acquired (date, cost, where, or from whom):

_____

_____

_____

The specific problem is:

_____

_____

_____

2. I am asking for this corrective action:

_____

_____

_____

3. Find the person to talk with. (List here by name, title, phone, and address all of the people who are in item 4 below.)

_____

_____

_____

_____

4. My efforts (record all contacts with the company, listing date, time, person, request, and result):

_____

_____

_____

_____

_____

10

How to Confront a Person Who Has Lied or Been Unjust to You

You know with certainty that your best friend lied to you. What do you say? And how?

Your neighbor is back for the third time this week asking to borrow a small amount of food. Money's not the problem. She's just been too busy to go to the store, she says. Kind-hearted you—you dole out half a loaf of bread with a smile as anger rumbles within you.

At the grocery store (you go there more often since you've been feeding the neighbors!) another customer starts wedging his cart into line ahead of yours. The anger rumbles again.

In the words of Carson Robison, a country singer of many years ago, "Life gets tedious, don't it?"

That's especially true for people like us who are inclined at times to be nicer to others than to ourselves. Nice guys don't always finish last, but sometimes they do so much to help other people get ahead they don't have enough energy to finish the race, themselves! Does that make sense?

This chapter is about situations in which the interests of another person crash into what is good for you. It is especially written for those persons who find it hard to resist pushy, insensitive behavior. There are many of us. We dislike standing up against such actions, with the result that we are taken advantage of. And anger rumbles.

When Sir Walter Raleigh put his coat on the puddle for the queen to walk across, he took it off first. That's smarter than some of the things we've done, huh?

This book advocates being nice. But I would wish for all of us that we would spread the welfare evenly—that we could be as considerate of our own needs as we are of the needs of others. Without guilt; with confidence. That can happen for you as you adopt the principles and methods of the easy way.

Wrong Turns

As usual, we identify the wrong turns first, although I'll bet they are already familiar to you.

For example, there's the wrong turn of retaliation. Human nature always nudges us in that direction. The person who has allowed others to take advantage of him or her—the rather unassertive person, I should say—is likely to retaliate in some indirect fashion. An example that comes immediately to mind (because I heard about it just an hour ago) illustrates this.

A resident in one of the dwellings where we provide emergency housing for the homeless broke the taillights out of one of the company vehicles. This apparently served to discharge the rumbling of that person's anger after being called to account about continuing violation of a rule.

When unassertive people do communicate, retaliation may leak into the conversation. It is frightfully easy to reject the person instead of just rejecting the person's behavior or attitude. It is easy for anger to propel us into ugly words or vehemence in a conversation.

Obstacles

What makes these situations difficult? The first obstacle is the fear of rejection. You want people to like you, don't you? Of course! We all do. The most common reason for giving in too easily to the demands of people is that we are afraid we will lose their love, friendship, or admiration if we refuse to give them what they ask. The fact is, even the people who would abuse us do not respect us for letting ourselves be taken advantage of. As for friendship with those who mooch and manipulate, who needs it?

The second obstacle is our anger. If being rejected by others is threatening to us, consider how much more painful it is to us when we reject ourselves. But this is exactly what we do if we let people take advantage of us. I believe that rejection always generates anger within us. Rejection of ourselves is rejection that we cannot escape. Better for me that *you* reject me, painful as that might be, than that *I* reject myself.

But our anger makes us unsure that we can have a constructive conversation. It shouts at us that we should not even try. It tells us—lying—that trying to make things better will only make them worse.

The third obstacle is the possibility that our values may be different. I don't know exactly what you might think. If you ask me for a ride home from work that takes me a mile out of my way, I don't know if that seems like a big favor to you or a small favor. So it is harder for me to estimate how you might react if I turn you down. The futility of trying to make that assessment shows why our decision should not be made on the basis of how we think the other person is going to act. Instead, we should decide on the basis of what we are able reasonably to invest in others without diminishing the efforts we must make for ourselves.

Fourth, giving in becomes a way of life, and with it there's always a sense of hopelessness. It takes a healthy measure of personal initiative and emotional energy to change the pattern. Those who have been in the pattern a long time may need outside help to do it.

Recognize the Costs of Giving In

People who live with a willingness to be taken advantage of accumulate a burden of anger and resentments. This burden is very difficult to live with. Stifled anger finds its way into physical problems: headaches, sleep difficulties, muscular tension, and stomach and intestinal disorders.

When someone realizes he or she has given in, and then realizes the costs of giving in, there is generally a loss of self-respect.

We need to realize that no one ever gets all the votes, that no musical group has all the songs on the top-forty list, that no athlete makes the all-star team every year. We need to remember that it is okay if some people don't like us. And most of all, we need to realize that giving in has not brought the peace of mind we hoped for—and it never will.

There is a big difference between giving and giving in. Giving is voluntary; giving in is having something taken away from us. Giving raises self-esteem; giving in leads to self-loathing. Giving builds bridges; giving in builds walls. Giving brings peace; giving in brings resentment. We will be able to do more giving if we do less giving in.

A Map

First you must accept that it is right and proper for you to resist abuse that is offered to or imposed upon you. You needn't even bother going forward in this chapter until you have settled in your mind that you will be better off resisting abusive requests and behaviors than giving in to them. Then, with that settled, follow this sequence.

1. *Describe the violation.* Get it together in your own mind so you can talk with the other person clearly and concisely.

2. *Describe your expectation.* What are you looking for from the other person? Define this in your mind so you can talk about it easily. Is it simply a matter of saying no, or at this point is it reasonable for you to expect some kind of redress for the abuse that has already happened? This chapter assumes the latter. What will you ask for?

3. *Get clout.* What can you do to force the person to fulfill what you are asking for? What consequence might there be for not fulfilling your request?

Two kinds of consequences to the abusing person result from his or her behavior: (1) making restitution and/or fulfilling some kind of penalty, and (2) the change in your behavior toward him or her that protects you from abuse in the future. You must look around and figure out how you can enforce these consequences. What's available? Perhaps nothing. Perhaps something is available, e.g., police involvement, but it is not practical.

With things settled in your own mind, you are prepared to talk with the person. Describe the offense and ask for its correction. If necessary, confront him or her with the consequences, and describe how things will be different in the future. Some familiar communication vehicles will be useful in this.

Communication Vehicles in Resisting and Repairing Abuse

Initial resistance uses the communication vehicle of saying no, described in detail in chapter 7. Consult that chapter if necessary.

To introduce your feelings about what has happened in the past and your expectations for the future, the I-statement pattern is very useful. You also may describe the consequences of failing to abide by the limitations you are setting—an ultimatum. Let's see how these might be used by reading some examples:

1. A good friend lied to you.

Easy-Way Response: It is quite painful to me to have discovered that you lied to me. It hurts quite deeply, not just because it changes how we get along in this particular situation, but I'm afraid it will continue to disrupt our friendship for quite a while in the future. Right now, I am interested in hearing your feelings and thoughts about how the this situation can be remedied.

(Comment: Notice the I-statements. Let's assume that the friend genuinely apologizes. Then Easy Way might continue . . .)

Easy-Way Response: It means a lot to me to hear your apology, which I have confidence in. I'm optimistic about the future of our friendship. I have to say candidly, though, that I expect to find it difficult to trust you as I have in the past, at least for a while. I hope you will not take offense if I seem to double-check things you say, or do other things of that sort. I'm not at all sure how I will be influenced by this, but I thought I ought to say that.

(Comment: Again, Easy Way uses an I-statement and related reporting about how the incident is likely to disrupt the relationship in the future.)

Now, let's suppose the other person was defensive and resistant instead of being cooperative.

Easy-Way Response: It seems to me as though right now you are justifying the lie you told me, and that makes me exceedingly sad. It's difficult for me to conceive of having a friendship that is good for either of us if we cannot fully rely on what we hear from the other person. I am committed to being 100 percent honest in what I say to you. If I fall short of that, I want to be held accountable. I need to hear the same integrity from the other person in an intense friendship—the sort of friendship we have had in the past and the kind I would like in the future. Without the confidence in its integrity, though, I see no future for our friendship.

(Comment: Note again the use of I-statements and the closing ultimatum, which is laid on the table gently, but very clearly. It is quite different than giving an ultimatum such as, "It sounds like you're telling me that you will lie to me any time you want to, and if that's the way it is, then I'm done with you." These two ultimatums say about the same thing but are radically different in style, and will harvest radically different results.)

2. The neighbor is back asking again to borrow food.

Easy-Way Response: I'm quite uncomfortable with how often you have been asking to borrow food. While you have not asked for very much at any one time, this is the third time this week. Each time, you have talked about repaying, but so far you have not done that. At this point I choose not to loan you anything more until you have repaid what you have borrowed up to this point.

(Comment: Again, Easy Way uses an I-statement, including a clear description of expectation, without apology for declining the request.)

3. At the grocery store check-out line another customer tries to get in line in front of you.

Easy-Way Response: Excuse me, but I believe your place in line would be right behind me, *or,* perhaps you didn't notice that I'm in line here.

If he continues to nudge in, get clout. Enlist help by saying, as loudly as necessary, "Cashier! Am I correct in thinking that you will be serving people in this line on a first-come, first-served basis?"

(Comment: Will that last one work? Well, it worked for me a few weeks ago. I didn't like doing it, but doggone it, I think those of us who enjoy civilized society are

obligated to help maintain it. So we have to do chores
like this once in a while.)

4. You are talking on the phone to someone who won't, won't, won't get off the line. What do you do?

Easy-Way Response: It's been good of you to call. I can only talk for one more minute, so we must wind down the conversation. [If that doesn't wrap it up, try:] That minute is gone and I must hang up now. We'll talk again another time. Goodbye. [Then hang up.]

At the beginning of a conversation with a person who is known to talk much too long, you can state how long you can talk. Say, "I can talk for five minutes, but no longer than that. What's on your mind?" Stick to it. Or say, "You're saying a lot of interesting things, and I hear your enthusiasm for what you are talking about. We won't be able to talk longer, because I must get off the phone and do some other things. It was nice of you to share your thoughts with me. Goodbye."

5. You are at a basketball arena where smoking is not permitted. A fan next to you lights a cigarette.

Easy-Way Response: Perhaps you're not aware that smoking is not permitted in the arena, *or,* is smoking permitted here?

Suppose the fan snickers and continues to smoke. Try saying, "I see that smoking is not permitted. Notice the sign over there? I'd like you to not smoke." If there's still no action, try, "If you put that out now, I won't have to call an usher."

6. Friends unexpectedly drop off their children to have you baby-sit them.

Easy-Way Response: I can watch the kids for one hour, but no longer than that, *or,* if I had children for you to baby-sit, we could trade times. But since I don't, what do you suggest that you do in exchange for what I'm doing for you?

Summary

Taking care of these relational chores is a lot like a cattle rancher keeping fences mended. The fence doesn't produce meat to take to market, but it protects the meat that is being produced.

It is not fair for you to enable people to abuse you because it teaches them bad habits. Nor is it fair to you, because it diminishes the quality of your life and reduces your capacity to give to those to whom you have primary obligations.

As you maintain your fences, you will treat those who would break them down with respect. While keeping the fences in good order takes some nerve and discipline, it is far easier than the havoc that you must deal with if you allow marauders to raid your pastures.

PERSONAL ACTION PLAN

1. Make sure you're convinced that you should reject this abuse from others. If you're not convinced, review the section in this chapter on the costs of giving in.

2. Define the violation: (person) _____
(situation)_____
_____

3. What do you want to accomplish? (To just say no this time? Or do you also wish the other person to remedy past abuse?) List what you want from him or her:
_____
_____

4. What appropriate means of enforcement are available to you in this situation? List them:
_____
_____

5. Write how you could say no to the request.
_____
_____

6. Write an I-statement that describes how you feel about the request.
_____
_____

I'm convinced it is better for me—and others—if I do not allow them to take advantage of me. I want to give, not give in. I'll fix the old problems that need to be fixed, and with kindness and respect I will protect myself in the future.

(signed) _____

(date) _____

11

How to Reject Gossip and Other Trash Talk

"It's shocking. It's titillating. It's a juicy story about someone you know. Right here and now, I've got the gossip that will knock you off your feet. Wait'll you hear this. . . ."

"This may be the grossest racial joke of all time, but I know you'll love it. It's about. . . ."

"I just need a little help from you. Nothing wrong, not very wrong, at least. Okay, so it's a little illegal, but if anybody gets in trouble it will be me, not you. But I can't do it without your help, so whatta ya say?"

And this has been pouring into your ear for twenty minutes, "I've always been on top. I was on top in high school—sports, grades, socially, you name it. I'm the best in my company. I was the favorite kid in my family. I was born to be a winner."

Trash talk. It comes in a dozen different packages. Sometimes it seems to come from a dozen directions at once. We might give trash talk a milder label—inappropriate communication. It could be defined differently by different people, but let's list some popular types:

1. *Rumor and gossip.* It's a rumor if people are talking about the organization, gossip if they are talking about *you.* Either way, it erodes trust and creates friction.

2. *Chronic complaining.* Do you know people who are grumpy so much of the time you want to run when you see them coming? What is it like to be around that sort of person? What is it like to *be* that sort of person? And what do we do to keep from getting smothered under the wet blanket of doom and gloom when he or she comes around?

3. *Hurtful activity.* This includes requests to join in on something that may hurt others or be illegal, immoral, stupid, or rude.

4. *Excessive bragging.* This is similar to chronic complaining in that it primarily hurts the person who is doing it. But don't you get sick of it?

5. *Overdependence.* Some people ask us to do things for them that they are fully capable of doing themselves. This, it seems to me, is inappropriate, because if we do it we enable the person to remain childish.

6. *Hostile humor and other degrading talk.* This category includes sarcasm, racial slurs, and vulgarity. Most vulgarity originates in hostility.

7. *Nonstop talking.* At a social gathering I ran into an acquaintance I had not seen for many years. He approached me from across the room, talking as he walked toward me. He continued chattering about himself at a rapid pace for five or six minutes. I couldn't have gotten a word in between two of his with a sledgehammer. During this deluge, which was frightfully boring, he said one thing that really made sense: "People tell me I still talk too much. I know they're right." But he continued to talk, and was still talking—to himself—as I excused myself

and walked away, leaving a one-sided conversation I didn't savor, wouldn't save, and would hate to relive. Trash.

In each of these categories, by definition, someone is being hurt. That's why I group them together and call them trash.

The Obstacle

These situations are difficult to deal with. In group after group of human-relations training sessions I have conducted, people have told me this is their most awkward relationship situation to handle, especially with friends. The reason it is tough to handle is because it is a "gray" area of right and wrong—an area in which one person's definition of trash may be different than another's. You think the joke is clean, I think it's dirty. Or I think the ethnic remark is cute, you think it's racist. Our values are different. So we tend to let these things go, not being willing to run the risk of offending the other person or taking the chance of feeling out of place.

I think we agree that each of these types has the potential to be quite destructive. We agree, no doubt, that we ought resist these communication patterns. Our first step is to avoid the wrong turns.

Wrong Turns

The basic wrong turn is to join in. The subtle way to join in is to remain silent. The old adage applies: "Silence gives consent." Silence, in the face of wrongdoing, is approval. If this were a major criminal act, the silent person would be an accomplice. But these violations of "gray" standards don't attract much attention. Should they be taken more seriously than they are? I think so.

The other wrong turn is to join in more actively. Who has not enjoyed hearing some ugly gossip? Fun! But who among us has not been hurt by being gossiped about? Not as much fun, is it?

If these communication types are trash, we need a map to avoid the wrong turns.

A Map

Here is a simple, straight-to-the-goal map that is easy to talk about but hard to practice. The map is this: *politely decline to take part in it.*

It's easy to decline, and it's usually fairly easy to be polite, but to put these two together is another thing! It may be difficult—it is—but any other approach means that the inappropriate talk or behavior will probably continue.

Okay, you say, if it's difficult, how can it be the easy way? Because taking the bull by the horns is a whole ton easier than letting it go. Otherwise, this is the bull that will run you down and stomp on you. If it's not the easy way, it is at least the easiest way.

Our strategy is to continue to affirm the other person as a person of worth, and to praise all of his or her appropriate behavior. We do this even as he or she has forced us to hold ourselves at a distance from the trash talk or behavior. This combination of affirming the person while rejecting the behavior was illustrated beautifully in chapter 6 in Steve's confrontation of Carl. You may want to review that, thinking about this tactic of encircling the other person with affirmation of his or her worth even as you push away that person's inappropriate behavior.

Let's have an example that makes a couple of wrong turns, then follows our map. Then we will become more specific about the communication vehicles that are used.

Examples of Wrong Turns—and Corrections

A co-worker says to you, "I can't believe who they just hired. I went to high school with that clown and, well, I can tell you plenty about him. Knowing him from way back as I do, I can tell you just what we're in for." Here are some responses to consider:

Wrong-Turn Response: I guess you can.

(Comment: That's polite, but it does not decline to participate. In fact, it leaves the impression that you are willing to hear more, so it's a wrong turn. Stopping

*inappropriate communication requires a firm refusal
to listen to it.)*

Wrong-Turn Response: Don't tell me anything. I'm not interested in any cheap gossip!

*(Comment: This one certainly declines to participate
but is, itself, so rude that it isn't helpful. You are not
very likely to influence someone if you make him or
her feel angry or offended. Thus, our goal is to be both
clear and polite. This response was not polite—another
wrong turn.)*

Easy-Way Response: That doesn't particularly interest me. I'll meet him when he starts working. . . . Say, how did your vacation go last week? I heard you had a good time.

*(Comment: This one fits the rule—it draws the line on
the trash, but welcomes talk on an okay subject.)*

Easy-Way Response: Well, I guess I'll wait and get acquainted with him first-hand. I'd be a little uncomfortable talking about him now. . . . How is your new project going? Last week you were really excited about it.

*(Comment: Good! Again, we follow the rule: push aside
the gossip, but invite discussion that is constructive.)*

Vehicles of Communication in Responding to Trash Talk

First, some pointers related to the "politely" part. Remove condemnation and punishment from the nonverbal channels. Your tone of voice should be calm and easygoing. Facial expression should be fairly neutral. Eye contact should be direct, but not piercing or hostile.

In the "decline" part, you need to say something that clearly indicates that you are unwilling to get involved in this type of discussion. Your words must give a clear, definite rejection. Keep this part brief, and avoid harsh words such as "dumb," "awful," "troublemaker." Also, avoid similar demeaning talk about the talker—which itself would be trash talk. Do not be apologetic about the "decline" part. Avoid smiling as you decline.

You wish to decline just the behavior, not your complete involvement with the person. So keep the conversation going in a positive way to show your interest in the person and your acceptance of him or her. As you move the conversation on to other things, don't jump in so quickly or so lightly as to deny the point you have made about declining. If you don't move the conversation along there is likely to be an awkward silence (which the speaker may fill with more trash) and your rejection of the other person's behavior may seem to him or her as complete rejection. At this point you can smile and be as animated as you wish.

The I-statement style can be useful here, as you will see from examples that follow.

More Examples of How to Respond to Gossip

Gossip: Their house is such a mess I can smell it from my yard! Not only that, but. . . .

Easy-Way Response: Before you go on, Bruno, I should say that I feel kind of uncomfortable hearing about them. I'd prefer if we could talk about something else—your trip last week, for instance.

(Comment: Simple map, isn't it? Politely decline, move on. Note the clear-cut I-statement.)

Nonstop Talker: [After ranting on for fifteen minutes] Yaketty-yak. Yaketty-yaketty-yaketty-yak-yak. Yak-yak-yaketty-yak. Yaketty-yak.

Easy-Way Response: Excuse me, Dorcina, but I'm getting a little frustrated. It's getting hard for me to keep up my interest in the conversation when I don't have a chance to contribute my thoughts, too. It would be a lot more enjoyable for me—for both of us, I think—if we could share in the talking. What are your thoughts about that?

(Comment: Again, some I-statements introduce a direct suggestion about doing things another way. Asking for an answer to the request raises the intensity.)

Speaker Expressing Bigotry: Them people talk about their ethnic pride, to which I say, "Bull!" What do they have to be proud over? Laziness? Stupidity?

Easy-Way Response: You seem to have pretty strong feelings about some things, and I'm willing to try to understand your feelings and ideas if that can be done without running people down. Otherwise I'd rather talk about other things.

(Comment: The trash talker shows a lot of angry energy, so the easy-way response is careful not to reject the talker as a person. But, the response clearly puts a limit on the kind of conversation that will be shared.)

Gossip: She told me to not say anything, but I don't mean harm to her by telling you about it. It's too funny to keep quiet, so I'll tell you, even if. . . . Well, anyway, what she did was, she. . . .

Easy-Way Response: Excuse me for interrupting you, but you seem to have mixed feelings about breaking confidence with her, and that makes me uneasy, too. Perhaps all three of us would be better off if you and I talked about something else instead. Would you tell me about your hobby of . . . ?

(Comment: This response is very clear, but it's polite, isn't it? Never, never, offend a gossip! Changing the subject can be rude, but in the case of trash talk we change the subject because: (1) it decisively shows that we wish to talk about other things, and (2) it keeps us engaged with the other person so they know that we are not rejecting him or her as a person.)

Chronic Complainer: [Stands at the window and says, for the third time in the last hour] Rain, rain, rain! I get so sick of it!

Easy-Way Response: It *is* tiresome to you, isn't it? But venting your frustration doesn't change the weather, and it has become tiresome to me to hear. If you wish to talk about something, please talk about something else.

(Comment: Wouldn't it be tempting to reply, "Complain, complain, complain! I get so sick of it"? Instead, the easy way gives a mirroring response—"tiresome to you"—and an I-statement.)

Overdependent Person: Look! I'm only seventeen years old. You shouldn't expect me to wake up in time for school by myself.

Easy-Way Response: Yes, that's exactly what I expect, because you are fully capable of doing so. I am not willing to treat you as though you were unable to take care of yourself. If I babied you, I would feel that I were not treating you with respect. I know what you can do and I admire you for that. That's why I would not let you settle for being less as a person.

(Comment: This statement shows a clear rejection of the unhealthy overdependence, with affirmation about the person.)

Someone Planning Hurtful Activity: I say if he's dumb enough to leave his car keys lying around, we ought to use 'em. He'll never know!

Easy-Way Response: I'm uncomfortable with the direction you're going with that, and want no part of it. I'll do something else with you now, but only after you put the keys back.

(Comment: Reject the action, accept the person. And do it politely. Simple map.)

Why This Seems to Be a Sensible Approach

Now that you've seen some examples, let me suggest why I think the easy-way approach is best in these situations:

1. While there is some risk, the risk is minimal. And this approach is less risky than the alternatives.

2. These communication patterns are dangerous. Our map gives us a response style that reduces harm to the person who is being inappropriate, and also to innocent parties and organizations where these things occur.

3. It affirms the worth of the person even while it rejects that person's inappropriate behavior.

4. Taking initiative to oppose that which is inappropriate is good for us.

A Small Amount of Risk Is Worth It

With this approach we seek to deal firmly with the trash and gently with the person. Even so, it may result in a bit of embarrassment for the person with trashy behavior. That embarrassment is just the natural consequence of their behavior, so we'll let the person live with that and hope he or she learns from it. While there is some risk with this approach, the potential for harm is greater if we don't do it.

Shortcut

To make it easier for the other persons, we shift the conversation to a subject they like. As they take our cue to talk about their hobby, vacation, proudest moment or whatever, the communication vehicle of mirroring will help us draw them out. Mirroring, as you know, provides an atmosphere in which the other person feels quite accepted, which softens any embarrassment that may have occurred.

Summary

Although we may be timid about standing against this kind of trash talk and resisting it may lead to some embarrassment for the inappropriate person, the rule is a good one and is the easiest way out of these situations. Doing anything else only keeps the problem alive.

Failure to resist trash means that more trash will blow into the yards of our lives. I don't want to live by a dumping ground, and I don't want you to have to, either. Let's agree, you and I, that we will resist trash talk. If enough of us say no to conversational garbage, the whole world will smell better.

PERSONAL ACTION PLAN

How do you get better at rejecting gossip? Practice. If you'll do a few in writing, you'll become able to respond the easy way on your feet when the time comes. Think of an incident when someone started talking trash, or invited you to take part in trash behavior. Write down the statement as accurately as you can, then write a response that follows the easy-way rule: *politely decline to take part in it.*

1. He (or she) said: _____

_____

_____

Easy-Way reply to 1: _____

_____

_____

2. He (or she) said: _____

_____

_____

Easy-Way reply to 2: _____

_____

_____

3. He (or she) said: _____

_____

_____

Easy-Way reply to 3: _____

_____

_____

My plan is to politely *decline to take part in trash talk.*

(signed) _____

(date) _____

12

How to Squelch
an Unwanted
Office Romance

After work, Brenda found a single red rose under the windshield wiper of her car.

She was puzzled.

The next day she found a computer-printed note on her office desk. It read, "You are the classiest woman in the office. You carry yourself with the regal bearing of a queen. Your vitality and congeniality are models for us all and I admire your intelligence. I hope we will become good friends. Very good friends. Bye for now, from a fan in the stands who thinks you are wonderful and would like to join you on the playing field."

Brenda was uneasy and annoyed.

The next day she found a fancy box of expensive chocolates in her desk drawer. A printed card taped to the box said
simply, "In friendship."

She was frightened and angry.

Rightfully so. She managed her response to the incidents
well, as you will read later in the chapter, and the mysterious
intrusions abruptly stopped.

But it made coming to work difficult. She found herself
suspicious and guarded in her relationships with all of the men.
Then she went through a phase of wondering if "Fan in the
Stands" was a woman. She had several sessions with a coun-
selor to discuss her anger and issues of identity. It was three
months before things settled back into a comfortable routine
and she felt like her cheerful and friendly self again.

She usually ate lunch in the office cafeteria with three work
friends. One day, delayed by a long phone call, she got there
later than usual. When she arrived, Tom, from the marketing
department, had just joined them. The other three soon left.

After some ordinary gab Tom said, "I hope you don't mind
my bringing it up, but I want you to know that I felt badly
about that nonsense a few months ago. I'm just glad the jerk is
gone."

Brenda gasped. She felt herself redden and the old tension
returned. "You know . . . ? You know who . . . ?"

Tom hesitated. "Uh, oops. I just assumed . . . I shouldn't
have . . . but thought they would have told you that you didn't
need to worry about . . . if you did, which I think would be
natural . . . but the guy is out of the picture now."

She leaned forward, as if to reach for a calming breath on
the other side of the knot in her stomach, found it, and leaned
back with a long, slow sigh. Then, moving close, she said in a
pinched whisper, "Who?"

"You deserve to know if I know," Tom said, "and you
should have been told through channels. You sure you . . . ?"

"Yes."

"Bert, in auditing. Real quiet guy with beady little eyes and
squirrel face. He's gone now. You'll never see him again."

Brenda had known him only by recognition.

"We called him 'Dirty Bertie,' Tom continued, "from a magazine that fell out of his briefcase once. He was hooked on telephone sex, too. The dumb guy made calls from the office phone. What a nut case!"

"Where . . . ?"

"Out of here forever. Gone back to his home state, I understand. Maybe they didn't tell you for fear you'd hold the company legally liable or something, but frankly, if I had been in charge of this I would have handled things for you quite differently. I'll bet it was real hard to go through what you did." He leaned across the table and touched her arm gently for just a moment. "You deserve to have your mind at rest."

They held eye contact and the tension ebbed. Brenda slowly massaged the fingers of her left hand one after the other and said thoughtfully, "Thanks. I didn't want to think about it today, but it helps to know."

Tom joined the group for lunch the next day. Affable and a good listener, he fit in well with the others and within a few weeks the usual four at the table became a cozy, convivial five. Bert was never mentioned.

Brenda knew from the warmth in Tom's eyes, and from the tingle in her heart, that there was a special bond between them. She liked that; yet she abhorred it. Tom was all she wanted in a man, save one thing: he was not single. She wanted no romantic overtures from him.

Some months later, Tom asked Brenda into his office for a short work-related conference. He closed the door, then sat on the edge of his desk close to where she stood. They had been selected to attend a two-day conference on "wellness and stress reduction in the workplace" at a resort a few hundred miles from their city, he explained.

"We'll gather ideas to bring back and use here. It will be good for all the people in the company. We will create a task force here, and develop some programs and maybe some policy changes that will make life better for everyone in the company. That's a win-win deal, and it's worth doing."

He reached to her shoulder and rubbed it tenderly. "But the best part is that you and I can have some quality time together. Now, I'm ready to make the arrangements. Should I get one room or two?"

Brenda took his hand in both of hers, gently turned it palm up and stroked his open palm. Then, lightning quick, she picked up the picture of his wife and children from his desk, closed his hand over the edge of it, and left.

An Obstacle

This chapter's problem comes with different faces. First there are the Berts—men who have not learned to talk or relate with women by mature means. They lack basic skills and attitudes that promote ordinary social involvement. They seek fulfillment of their relationship needs and sexual desires through means that are at best clumsy and unrewarding, and that gravitate in the direction of thoughts and behaviors that are asocial, self-defeating, immoral, illegal, and dangerous to other people and to themselves. If they wander long enough in that direction, as they will without help, they *always* reap the most miserable of harvests.

Next there are the Toms. The superficial social skills of these men are superb, but their psychological/spiritual selves are as lacking in bedrock maturity as are the Berts'. To the casual observer, the Toms seem to have it together, but they are driven by the same unquenchable hunger to be assured of their worth as the Berts are. As they wander from one infatuation to the next they wreak havoc around them and are forever thirsty for the clear, cool water of love.

It is not within the scope of this chapter to describe the origin or resolution of these conditions. Our purposes are to warn you that the unsought romantic can present himself or herself in many guises. Some of them are quite appealing, but they can be a real menace. The goal of this chapter is to help you become more confident and effective should you need to stifle one of these characters.

About This Chapter

Two things made writing this chapter a bit different than the others. First, in this chapter that deals with conflict between the sexes, I wanted to make it easy for you to keep track of the cast of characters. But I wanted to avoid sexism in my writing style. Both men and women are sometimes inappropriate in pursuit of romance, but statistically it is far more prevalent for men to take the offensive role. (Offensive in more than one way!) So it is easier for most of our readers to read the chapter if it is written with the man consistently in the aggressor's role. Understand that the reverse occurs—there *are* female Berts and Toms—and that the same principles and tactics apply.

Another unique difficulty was settling on a term to describe the man (or woman) who engages in this behavior. Labels used elsewhere didn't appeal to me. "Wolf" and "Romeo" are sexist and seem a bit dated. To call this person a "flirt" did not seem strong enough, for flirting can be innocuous. To say "predator" seemed too severe for most of those whom you'd encounter, though there is a predatory aspect to the behavior we are describing, and deadly predators exist.

The term should be specific, unattractive, and negative without being extreme. What short term could I use to describe this overzealous flirting nerd? Ah-ha! There it was: a *flerd*.

The Underlying Problem

Want another reason why flerd is a good name for these characters? They suffer from a

    Fatal
    Lag in
    Emotional and
    Relational
    Development.

It's a serious condition. Flerds may not know they have it, but it's obvious to everyone else. They simply have not grown up enough to become aware of the effect they have on others, nor have they acquired a strength of identity that allows them to set aside the pursuit of their own desires and contribute toward the needs and desires of others. If that sounds like people who are somewhat infantile, you have the picture!

Wrong Turns

As usual, there are more ways to get off track than to stay on it. Here are some strategies that do not work for the people who need to squelch the flerds in their lives.

One mistake commonly made is to think that flerds are going to change their ways. Flerds don't reform readily. They change costumes in the hopes of capturing your attention, but a flerd's a flerd. He or she tries different ploys, just as a fisherman changes bait, but each play has a hook you shouldn't bite.

Making too much of the flerds' come-on is likely to backfire. If you reject them directly they may accuse you of misreading their signals or statements. They will do this to cover their embarrassment.

"You've got to be kidding!" a flerd gasps indignantly. "You're totally out of your mind. I wasn't suggesting *that*!" And he laughs through his lying teeth. You know he's a jerk, but he's made you feel like a fish flung to dry land, and you won't survive unless you get away from him and back to a better environment.

The biggest mistake you can make is to be rude to flerds. Although they are insensitive to *your* feelings, they are supersensitive to their own. They bruise easily and are inclined to overreact. If you make a scene, the flerd will remember it forever. Then what will you do if he or she becomes your boss, or the person you need to write a reference letter for you?

A person who is inept in pursuit is likely to be ugly in rejection. Hurt a flirt and you flirt with hurt. Your goal will be to stop the behavior and preserve your self-respect and reputation without being destructive to the flerd.

Don't complain or gossip about the flerd to others in the office. In doing so you may publicly humiliate the flerd. (This would give you a cheap thrill, I know, but don't worry; your secret is safe with me. I just hope you won't settle for a cheap thrill.) Little is worse than being put down in front of peers. If you cause that, even without setting out to do so, the flerd will get even. Complain only if necessary, and then with a careful process to your supervisor.

The Map

The approach that usually works best when fending off unwanted requests is to affirm the person and reject the person's behavior. We choose to say, in effect, "You are okay, but this particular request of yours is *not* okay."

In most situations the affirmation serves merely to reduce the pain the other person feels when we reject his or her behavior. But in the situation of squelching a flerd, the situation is more complicated because the affirmation is strongly desired. The flerd is in pursuit of self-worth, of significance, and of feeling valued by others. The sparkle of infatuation, the aura of a romantic interlude, the excitement of sexual conquest are merely trophies the flerd collects in an effort to establish that he or she is someone. A flerd is a cough drop that soothes a sore throat when what is needed is a cure for the disease. Flerds are but cotton candy for a case of malnutrition.

It just doesn't do, then, to affirm flerds. It only encourages them.

Vehicles to Use in Flerd Fending

Strong measures are needed, usually in combination. Here, in no particular order, are fifteen tactics that may be helpful when adapted to your situation.

- *"Don't tread on me."* When Brenda found the note on her desk, she didn't know what to do. She stewed about it overnight and came to work the next day with frazzled nerves, so that when she found the chocolates in her desk she was instantly furious. On impulse she grabbed the note and wrote on it, "Lost and found department. Who does this belong to?" She made a copy of it. Then, without being seen, she posted the original on the most prominent company bulletin board.

She worried over the chocolates that night, and talked the next day with the personnel director about both incidents. The personnel director had seen the note on the bulletin board but had left it there. A strongly worded memo from management that cited company policies on sexual harassment and rights of privacy was issued.

Because it blanketed the company, no one was publicly humiliated. Bert, not yet identified as the perpetrator, got the message that neither Brenda nor the company would accept the behavior that had gone on.

• *Use body language that says you're not interested.* Nonverbal signals that say, "No, I'm not available" are powerfully effective with minimal risk. There is less risk because you do not give the flerd something he or she can quote or sulk over. It can seem much less deliberate (and therefore much less rejecting) yet it gets the point across.

Examples of this kind of body language include giving very little eye contact and crossing your arms in front of you, a stance that communicates disinterest in relationship. When possible, orient your body away from the flerd—give him or her the "cold shoulder."

Make sure your body language is not giving two different signals. Be careful not to stand close to or brush against the flerd, or put yourself in a seductive posture.

• *Say, "Thanks, but no thanks."* Soften the blow to the flerd's ego by thanking him for his interest. You might say, "I feel complimented by your interest in me. That's very nice." Then move to a clear dismissal of any possibilities for the two of you, such as, "My interest in is another person," or "Flattered as I am, there aren't any possibilities for the two of us."

• S*ay, "Let me tell you about. . . ."* Boldly advertise your enthusiasm for the love of your life. If your expressions run to the point of boring the flerd, so much the better. Ask, "Have I told you how wonderful my boyfriend is?" Or rave, "I'm just wild about Harry, and he's just wild about me."

It is characteristic of flerds to be unsure of themselves and thus take the path of least resistance. This deflects them from those who have a romantic partner nearby. Flerds can't handle competition.

If you currently don't have a romantic interest, consider talking about your ideal partner. Emphasize those characteristics of your ideal that would be most repugnant to the flerd. This lets him discover he is not your type, and to conclude from that, that you're not his type after all.

• *Business is business.* Plunge your energy into your work. Keep all conversations with the flerd connected directly to business matters, and *only* business matters. Let it be known—by your actions—that your fervor for job-related concerns far exceeds your inclination for an office romance.

• *Keep the office door open.* Don't get into compromising situations with the flerd. Avoid, to every extent possible, getting in one-to-one situations with him. Don't get behind a closed door with him if you can avoid it. For example, if a luncheon or after-hours meeting is necessary, bring a colleague. Surround yourself with safety in numbers.

• *Shut the relational door.* A week before they went to the conference, Brenda talked to Tom. "I'm glad we're going to the conference. Thanks for booking my room for me. I'm planning to work hard there—all business. *All business.*"

"Me too," he said. "I'm sorry for coming on to you. Thanks for fending me off." She wasn't sure if he meant it, but she never had a problem from him again.

• *Compile a record.* If it becomes seriously repetitive or provocative, begin keeping a detailed record of the flerd's inappropriate behavior. Keep this at home and do not mention it to anyone. If everything else fails, you may, as a last resort, tell the flerd that you have been keeping a record of his advances in the event that you would need to file a formal complaint.

• *Play dumb.* If you pretend that you do not comprehend that he is initiating romance with you, he has a chance to back away.

• *Play tough.* When riding down the elevator one afternoon Brenda stood beside Rob, a paralegal who had been in a conference she had attended a few minutes earlier. She felt his hand around her waist and he whispered in her ear, "You're nice. Very nice."

She said, loudly, "This man's name is Rob. I won't mention the law office where he works, but you all need to know he just had his hands where they don't belong." The car was deathly quiet, and Rob would have gotten off while it was moving if he could have. He bolted from the car at its next stop, and the passengers applauded Brenda.

She was scared. And proud.

• *"If you knew . . ."* If the flerd is a "Felix Unger neatnik," describe yourself as an "Oscar Madison slob" at heart. Advertise the part of your life that is least appealing to the flerd. You imply, or may even say, "If you knew what I'm really like, you'd run to the nearest exit."

• *Don't talk with the flerd about your personal life.* Above all, don't be a compassionate listening ear to the flerd's problems. This is one kind of person and situation that you cannot positively reinforce. Again, the reason is that this is the kind of neurotic, emotional unloading that the flerd longs for. You're not the one to provide it.

• *Remember them?* If the flerd is married, tell him how interested you are in meeting his wife. If social events give opportunity for you to meet her, tell the flerd about your enthusiasm for developing your own friendship with her. Nothing is more frightening to the flerd.

Similarly, talking about his children brings him back to reality. Ask about how he teaches values to his children or if he wishes his children to have monogamous marriages.

Brenda jolted Tom with a shock of "remember them" by picking up the picture of his wife and children.

• *Consider carefully whether to take the story home.* Be very careful when making a decision whether to tell your husband or wife about a flerd. Many people are ill-equipped to manage that kind of threat. The emotionally weakest among them may assume willingness on your part and use the imagined threat that you would be unfaithful to justify infidelity on their part. (*She's going to sooner or later,* the bogus thinking goes, *so I may as well do it now.*)

The best thing you can do to help fend off the flerd is for you and your spouse to create an extraordinary marriage for the two of you.

• *Take it to the top if you have to.* If the flerd becomes a menace, blow the whistle on him. You owe it to yourself, to the organization, and to the others who may be hurt. Don't you wish he had been put out of commission by one of those who had been hurt by him before he hurt you?

In Brenda's first situation, she went quickly to the personnel director the first time because she did not know who the flerd was. In the situation with Tom, she was disgusted but felt able to rebuff him on her own, even while at the seminar. But she wrote personal notes about it as soon as she left his office, just in case she would need them later.

Shortcut

In this situation, as in most, the best route to your goal is a straight line, and the most common reason for not traveling in a straight line is that you have not clearly defined your goal. If you have not decided what you want in a relationship or what you want in a person you are in relationship with, you will be distracted by second-rate invitations.

You will be likely to give conflicting signals—come here, go away, come here. These signals are consistent with your mood and mind because your mood and mind are changing—probably because you have not settled your goal. So if there is a shortcut to eliminate hassles in situations of this type, it is this: Define goals that are consistent with the best values and move toward them with vigor and without compromise.

Summary

Beware the flerd, the child in adult costume, who poses as a friend only to gather cheap gratifications and pour them into a bucket without a bottom, an ego with no boundaries. Deal with that person with firmness, giving respect but withholding empathy so as not to reward the inappropriate behavior. And may you find the love of your life who makes manageable all of the distractions and annoyances that, unbidden and unwelcome, enter your life.

PERSONAL ACTION PLAN

1. Have you defined your goal? What do you want in a romantic partner? Do you have a list of the top ten attributes of your ideal? As you define the criteria you seek in your special person, any approach will be helpful if it includes *both* qualities of character (e.g., honest) and activities (e.g., likes noncompetitive exercise). If you have never collected these thoughts, carry a three-by-five card with you for a couple of weeks and record your ideas. Gradually you can shape them into a list of "ten biggies" or "the essentials." However you do it, you need to define the standard.

2. Having defined the standard, how do the people you know compare with the standard? Measure!

3. If you have a problem person now, review the fifteen tactics in this chapter and choose three you can employ now. List the tactic, then describe how you will use it.

Tactic #1 _____

I will use it this way: _____

_____

_____ on or before (date) _____

Tactic #2 _____

I will use it this way: _____

_____

_____ on or before (date) _____

Tactic #3 _____

I will use it this way: _____

_____

_____ on or before (date) _____

This is my best plan, and I will follow it.

(signed) _____

(date) _____

13

How to Talk to a Friend Who Has Bad Breath, and Other Hazardous Duties

Isn't this topic high on your list of conversations you hope to never have? Maybe the only thing appealing about giving this bad news to a friend is that it would be easier than hearing it!

But there are many times when it would be beneficial to us—and to others—to tell them what they need to hear, even though they don't want to hear it. While this may be intimidating, you can do it and do it well, the easy way.

Beneficial Bad News

When the word "feedback" is used in human relations it means telling other people something about their effect on you or on others to help them learn about themselves. Feedback can be positive (e.g., giving compliments) or it can be negative (e.g., that they often interrupt the conversation rudely). We benefit from both.

Compliments are a lot more fun, but we need not think of negative criticism as a horrible thing to be avoided. We grow by changing the things we need to change, and we can't change them until we know about them. I like to call negative feedback "beneficial bad news."

Obstacles

Why is negative feedback so hard to give to others? There are several obstacles. If the feedback is about something that does not affect us directly, the obstacle may be our own indifference. Because we aren't affected much by the other persons' behavior, we simply don't get around to telling them what they need to hear.

If we think the other persons may react against us because we have embarrassed them with the feedback, the obstacle we may encounter is fear of their reprisal. In the fable, none of the mice wanted to tie the bell around the cat's neck, but they all wanted to hear the cat coming. That was the nature of those mice in that fable; it's the nature of many humans in real life, as well.

Then there are the situations in which the other person's behavior strikes us in such a personal way that we get angry about it. You are quite sure, for example, that he clips his fingernails and lets the trimmings drop on the carpet just to annoy you. Maybe it's a habit born out of ignorance or unrefined family examples, but you take it as hostility toward you. So instead of calm, reasonable feedback, you blast his ears off!

Some Indirect Approaches

For situations in the "bad-breath" category where the problem is simple and easy to define, an indirect approach may work. Here are a few ways to drop hints—to "leave the motor running in the car" in hopes the person will drive away with it.

• *Ask him or her to be your consultant.* I recall a person who worked as a public-relations representative for a large non-profit organization. While his personal relationships were excellent and his work was productive, the style of his clothing and his grooming were unacceptable. The president called him in to ask his opinions about a dress code for employees, especially those who met with the public. As they talked through this question, apparently it dawned on the man that he needed to make some changes, because he did.

Was it necessary to use the indirect approach? I don't know, but it worked.

• *Send them to school.* In organizations, it would take the form of attendance at a workshop that addresses the offensive behavior. Among friends, it takes the form of passing along a magazine article or giving a book. Frankly, I'm pessimistic about these efforts making much difference unless there is conversation about the problem, too.

• *Use a parable.* Sometimes the boss or a friend tells a story to teach a lesson. This is more personal than the seminar or book, and is more likely to work. Caution: Don't embarrass a person in front of others. Don't shift from an indirect group method to a direct personal method in the group. Conduct personal conversations in private.

• *Try the Easter bunny approach.* The package of breath mints or deodorant left for the person to find has a long history. Perhaps because this is more convenient than reading, and more dramatic, it seems to work more often. But again, the costs may be high. Doing this may be the action of one person, but the receiver of the confrontation may become self-conscious and uncomfortable around many others by not knowing where the confrontation came from. Also, there is no context of support and caring around it.

Some Foundational Thoughts

But giving beneficial bad news is rarely as difficult as we think it will be. You can learn to do it the easy way. And it will be useful. When people understand how they affect others, they can change. Those changes can benefit all the people in their lives.

How easy it is to receive feedback is closely related to the way in which it is given. Feedback is easiest to give if you listen thoroughly before you give it. If you know what you are talking about, and if you have been respectful and trustworthy to the person in the past it is much easier for them to receive what you say.

It is a lot easier to give and receive feedback about things that have happened long enough ago that there isn't much emotion attached to them anymore. You can jump all over me about the dumb things I did during junior high school, but please be kind when you tell me about today's blunder.

Telling other people about their behavior is a normal and valuable part of friendship and family life. To offer explanations about the underlying motivations—why someone does what he or she does—is outside the scope of what you should try. Leave out the "whys." They might be important in therapy, but not here.

The Map

There are nine landmarks on our map, each with a wrong turn. The chart below shows them all: easy-way styles (effective) and wrong turns (ineffective). These are in four groups, but there is no particular order. They are numbered just so you can connect the examples that follow with the items on the chart. The numbers do not represent the order in which they might appear in any other conversation.

Checklist for Giving Beneficial Bad News

Ineffective		*Effective*
1. Asks "why?" Condemns Judges Interprets	**Focuses on Target Behavior**	1. Describes the target behavior
2. Is general		2. Is specific
3. Is unrealistic		3. Is attainable
4. Little or no empathy is expressed	**May Include Content in Addition to Target Behavior**	4. Empathy is included in communication
5. The reason for giving feedback is not expressed		5. Reports giver's needs and feelings (I-statements)
6. Gets off track or stays superficial		6. Offers alternatives
7. "Hit and run"	**Style of Delivery**	7. Comments are checked and verified
8. Dogmatic Dictatorial		8. Tentative Flexible
9. Fosters overdependence Overly cautious Insensitive Punishing (harsh)	**Shows Respect**	9. Affirms the personhood of the other and praises positive behavior

Wrong Turns

Here is a conversation that takes nine wrong turns in a row. (You've *never* gone that far off track!) They follow the sequence in the chart. Compare each with the effective style that has the same number.

In this conversation, Mort, who hasn't read this book and doesn't know about the easy way, is talking with Fran. Mort has been listening long enough to be a little fed up with Fran's complaining. See if you think Mort is being helpful.

1. *Condemns*
MORT: You complain all the time about being lonely. Blaming everyone else for your problems is pretty immature! You're getting paranoid!
FRAN: Listen to you! You're proving my point that everybody's against me!

2. *Too general*
MORT: I didn't say that everyone was against you. It's just that you're making your own life miserable.
FRAN: What do you mean by that?

3. *Unrealistic*
MORT: I mean if you don't want to be lonely, why don't you do something that will make you popular? Get on TV, for example.
FRAN: Good grief! That's a ridiculous suggestion! Why don't you ask me to fly to the moon or something?

4. *No empathy*
MORT: Well, you've got a problem and you need to get over it.
FRAN: I'm doing the best I can.

5. *Reason for giving feedback is not shown.*
MORT: Huh!
FRAN: What's that supposed to mean?

6. *Digresses*

MORT: It can mean whatever you want it to mean. You know, lots of people are getting a lot more out of life than you are. Rich and Diana are happy. By the way, did you hear that they're going on vacation next week? They're going to the Adirondacks, which are really beautiful. Have you ever been there?

FRAN: I told you I'm lonely, but that doesn't mean I'm not getting enough out of life.

7. *"Hit and run"*

MORT: You're talking in circles. I explained it's your own fault. I can't talk about this forever. I have things to do. If you want to get over this problem you have to do what you have to do. There's nothing more to say.

FRAN: But that's hard for me to do.

8. *Dictatorial*

MORT: Well, you've got to do it, that's all. There isn't any other way. A person either does what has to be done or it's just tough luck for that person. You have to make up your mind if you're going to get with it or not.

FRAN: You make it sound like it's real easy, but it isn't. At least not for me.

9. *Punishing style*

MORT: If you don't shape up, you're headed for big trouble. You're never going to make it in life living the way you are now. You're turning into a loser.

FRAN: Look, I'm doing okay. At least I don't go around butting into other people's lives like you do! I've had enough of this conversation. Goodbye!

(Comment: Oh, Fran, it's me—Rich, the author. Please listen to me for just a moment. I'm sorry for letting Mort

talk to you. I didn't know he was that clumsy! If you'll trust me again, please talk to my good friend, Easy Way, who's the opposite of Mort.)

Vehicles of the Easy Way

The conversation below illustrates nine effective elements that may be included when giving beneficial bad news. (You'll do it this well *all the time,* when you catch on to the easy way!) Again, the vehicles are in the order they appear on the chart, but in your situations you will pick and choose, using this and that in whatever order is best for the occasion.

1. *Describes target behavior*

EASY WAY: You've been talking a lot about your feelings of loneliness. I have an idea that I think fits in with what you've told me. Mainly, it's this: I have a hunch that you have more control over this loneliness than you're using, that how lonely you are is up to you.

FRAN: Oh, I don't think that's so at all!

2. *Specific*

EASY WAY: Maybe not, but perhaps I can be more specific. You said a few minutes ago that you were lonely all weekend, yet you were invited to a party Saturday and, in fact, I offered to pick you up on my way there. You didn't go.

FRAN: But I didn't know anybody else who was going to be there.

3. *Shows the target behavior is attainable*

EASY WAY: Except for me, yes. But it seems to me that in the past you have been successful at meeting new people.

FRAN: Yes, but it's hard for me to do that.

4. *Empathy*

EASY WAY: I guess it is kind of scary, or difficult, for you at the present time.

FRAN: Yes, it is.

5. *Shows the giver's needs and feelings.*

EASY WAY: I am uncomfortable seeing you do what I think is "copping out" on yourself. When you do that I get uneasy because I think it's not good for you.

FRAN: Well, maybe it isn't, but what else could I do?

6. *Offers alternatives*

EASY WAY: That's a good question. Meeting new people is one way of reducing your loneliness, but that's not all you can do. You might do more with the persons you already know—write letters, make more phone calls, invite them to do things instead of waiting for them to invite you.

FRAN: Yeah, I guess those things would help.

7. *Checks it out*

EASY WAY: Let me see if I understand: Does it make sense to you that maybe you actually are at least partly responsible for the way things are now? And that you could take more control to change things?

FRAN: Yeah, I'd agree with that.

8. *Tentative*

EASY WAY: Well, these have just been suggestions, of course, but maybe they'll get you thinking about some things.

FRAN: It has already. You know what? I think I'll throw a small party of my own—nothing big. I'll just invite a few people I know pretty well already— people who get along well with each other.

9. *Praises*

EASY WAY: That sounds terrific! And it really doesn't surprise me that you are deciding to do something about it right away.

FRAN: Thanks. Hey, you got any more ideas?

Shortcut

Both giving and receiving beneficial bad news is easier when the package is wrapped in praise—but only if the praise has been earned, the person knows that you know it has been earned, and if you genuinely want to offer it. A phony compliment is a flat tire, not a shortcut.

If you have not read the conversation between Steve and Carl in chapter 6 recently, it's worth reviewing now. Notice how frequently earned praise is intermingled with Steve's confrontation.

Summary

You are the wonderful person you are because people have helped you smooth out your rough edges. I suppose if a piano had feelings it wouldn't like being sanded, but a part of the beauty of a piano is its glassy smooth surface. That has been possible only by repeated sanding and rubbing.

People have done some rubbing and sanding on you; that's why you're becoming a "grand"! Do the same for others as skillfully as you know how.

PERSONAL ACTION PLAN

I will talk with (person's initials) _____
about _____

1. List the problems you know the other person has. This will help you put it in perspective and communicate empathy. _____
_____

2. List positive behaviors and characteristics of the person that you can mention to praise that person. _____
_____
_____

3. Identify behaviors or characteristics about which you plan to give feedback now. _____
_____

4. Why should you give this feedback? What business is it of yours? _____
_____

5. Write at least two I-statements to describe how you feel about this matter. _____
_____

6.List suggestions you could give the person to teach new behavior. _____
_____

7. Rehearse delivering the feedback. You can do it mentally by yourself, but if a lot is at stake it would be much better to talk and rehearse with a friend. Use the chart of effective styles as you rehearse.

This is my best plan. For their benefit, I will do it!

(signed) _____

(date) _____

14

How to Give and Receive Compliments

Maybe it seems odd that receiving compliments should be part of a book about hard situations. Compliments should always be fun, we might think. But many people feel awkward instead of comfortable around compliments, whether they are on the giving or receiving end. The result: Many deserved compliments are not given, and of those that are given, many are received in clumsy fashion.

Obstacles to Receiving Compliments Easily

You know from personal experience that some compliments are given for the wrong reasons. There are several types of phony compliments. For example:

• *Bait.* This is a compliment given by a person fishing for a compliment in return.

• *Motivator.* These words are given only to urge a person to work harder.

• *The Foot in the Door.* Used as an introduction to criticism—first the good news, then the bad news. Sincere compliments always soften the blow of criticism. But a phony compliment would not have been given had it not been for the task of reporting bad news.

• *The Band-Aid.* This is quick verbal first aid to cover up hurt inflicted on another. It is somewhat like putting a basket of flowers on your piano to hide the place I scratched it.

• *The Setup.* This cheap flattery softens you up so you can be manipulated. After we've been taken in by such trickery, we get a little more cautious. The fact is that most people are too suspicious about compliments and may reject them as phony when they are not.

Another reason people are sometimes reluctant to receive a compliment is that they do not want to accept a standard of high performance that they will have difficulty living up to in the future. Ouch!

A Common Wrong Turn When Receiving Compliments

I have met very few people who rate themselves as very adept or thoughtful in the skill of giving compliments. Even fewer are skilled at receiving them, yet many people are not aware of how unskilled they are. For some it may be the relationship activity they do worst.

A common response to a compliment is to call the compliment giver "stupid." Oh, it's not said that bluntly. It's done with false humility. What's wrong with this conversation?

COMPLIMENT: You really did a great job playing the piano at the party.

RESPONSE: Oh, it wasn't that good. I had an off night. I was missing notes and just stumbling through. My arpeggios were slow and brittle. It was terrible!

It seems the response is, in effect, "If you knew anything about music, you wouldn't have said such a dumb thing!"

A Map for Receiving Compliments Graciously

Most compliments are genuine. You usually get fewer than you deserve, so don't argue—accept them. Receiving a compliment is a very short trip with an easy map: Just gladly accept the gift.

A Vehicle for Receiving a Compliment

The best way to receive a compliment is simply to say, "thank you." You can hardly improve on that. If you want to say more, tell how the compliment makes you feel. Use an I-statement such as, "It really makes me feel good to hear that." Or say:

"That's nice to hear."
"It is very nice of you to say that."
"Thanks for mentioning that."
"It's kind of you to tell me."

Don't overreact out of fear of getting the big head. A few compliments aren't going to turn humble, wonderful you into an arrogant, obnoxiously proud person. Live so that you deserve compliments (which is the only way you'll get one that's worthwhile) and when you get one, enjoy the moment and move on to other good things in life.

The Shortcut for Receiving Compliments

When you are complimented, smile and say, "Thanks."

Wrong Turns in Giving Compliments

The no-nos have been identified already—the list of phony compliments that are obstacles in our road. We also need to avoid the wrong turn of dropping them for others to trip over.

Obstacles to Giving Compliments

If people tend to be leery about trusting compliments, is it safe to give them? Will people think we're phony simply because five out of the last six compliments they got from other people seemed phony to them? They might. But even if there may be a bit of risk in giving compliments, it is a risk worth taking because people want and need affirmation they have earned.

A Map for Giving Compliments Easily

Here's how you can keep risk to a minimum when giving compliments:
- Be sure the compliment is deserved.
- The compliment means more if the person knows you have been in a position to know whether or not it is deserved. If there is doubt, explain.
- Give the compliments you want to give. It doesn't mean you have to like the person. You may even be struggling with envy. Such circumstances may even enhance the value of the compliment to the receiver. But most of all—if you want to give it, give it; if not, don't.
- Say it in your own style. Keep it short and simple.
- To the best of your ability, give it for the other person's benefit, not yours.

A Vehicle for Delivering Compliments

The I-statement pattern works very well as a vehicle for delivering compliments. You simply state what the other person did and how you felt about it: "When you _____ I felt _____."

"When you sang the anthem, I felt inspired."

"The painting you exhibited is awesome!"

If you want to say a little more, add a "because": "When you _____ I felt _____ because _____."

"When you sang the anthem, I was inspired because you not only sang it well, but you sounded inspired by it, too."

"The painting you exhibited is awesome! Not only is it beautifully executed, but it brought back wonderful memories to me because it reminded me of my childhood."

A Shortcut to Giving Compliments the Easy Way

Giving a compliment need take only a word—a split second. Plus honesty.

The pastor of one of the healthiest, most vigorous churches I know says "fantastic" again and again and again. But it does not get tiresome to people because he says it to those who have earned praise, and he means it. Although I have not been around him much, he said it to me about something I'd done, and guess what: I felt fantastic!

So I began using the words "fantastic" and "wonderful" and "good for you" and "super" to people a lot more (but only when I meant it), and guess what: It turned into great fun! *Wonderful!*

Summary

Want to feel wonderful more often? Give compliments generously; receive them graciously. Pass them along. I will, too, and if we all do it when they are deserved maybe we can cover up the litter of gossip and other trash talk with a layer of beauty. Is it a deal? Good for you! You're fantastic!

PERSONAL ACTION PLAN

Receiving Compliments

I'm planning to live so that I earn compliments, not for that reason, but because that's the most sensible way to live. Therefore, when I am complimented, I will receive the compliment joyfully and gratefully by simply saying, "Thank you."

Giving Compliments

I want to be up to date in complimenting the people in my life who deserve a compliment from me. I will give these specific compliments by the date specified:

Person	About	Date
_____	_____	_____
_____	_____	_____
_____	_____	_____
_____	_____	_____
_____	_____	_____
_____	_____	_____

In addition, I intend to give at least one spontaneous compliment each day to deserving persons around me, whether I know them or not, or whether there's anything in it for me or not.

These are my aims for improving my attitudes and performance in giving and receiving compliments.

(signed) _____

(date) _____

15

How to Apologize

"Apologize?" he shouted. "No one does *that* any more!"

"Sure, I'll *say* I'm sorry, but I'll never *be* sorry."

"I'll apologize to her right after she apologizes to me."

People don't find apologizing very appealing, do they? For most people, it is usually very difficult.

Apologizing is the corrective for an offense against another person. It is an act of strength. It is evidence of the maturity you already have, and it helps build greater personal maturity. It has great benefits, but unless you're different than the rest of us, you'll hate to do it.

Obstacles to Apologizing

The great barrier to apologizing is embarrassment, or to use a word that is even uglier because it is more accurate, pride. We may mistakenly think apologizing is for the benefit of the other person. To some extent it is, but when you apologize *you* are the one who gets the greatest rewards: release from guilt and shame, and from fear that you will be found out to be less than perfect or that the other person will retaliate against you. Apologizing is the best defense against retaliation.

A Map for Apologizing

To apologize is to be sorry: to
Soon
Offer
Regret and
Restitution,
Yourself.
Let's consider these five elements one at a time.

• *Soon.* The earlier you do it the better. That is difficult, because it means a commitment to change the direction of your attitudes or change your behavior. But putting it off is difficult, too. Our minds begin to imagine the other person laughing at us or accusing us or talking about us. It doesn't pay to wait.

We may procrastinate in the hope that we will forget about it. We try to cover our discontent with layer after layer of excuses and frivolity, or maybe even good works, but there is no silencing the nagging shame when we know we have been unjust or unkind.

• *Offer.* An apology that is pulled out of you is only hollow words—worthless words. The value of an apology comes from the intention to change future behavior, and it can be only you who controls that. If you don't intend to change you're not really sorry. If you're *not* sorry, don't say you are, for that only adds phoniness, which is also wrong.

• *Regret*. This means you wish you hadn't and you won't in the future. The evidence of your regret is your intention to make your future behavior better than past behavior. The important part of an apology is not what you say, but what you mean. The words of your apology tell another person about your feelings, attitudes, and intentions, but what counts is how you live out that intention.

• *Restitution*. This is to do the best you can to compensate for the damage you've done, to seek to restore the situation back to the original condition. Sometimes you know exactly whom to go to and what to do. For example, John was driving from the Midwest to California when, in the middle of the night, he had a flat tire. He put on his decrepit spare tire and drove carefully into the next town. He found a car with good tires on a dark street and stole a tire. It was so good he thought, "why be wasteful?" and took another. A year later he went back, found the owner, and paid. Hard? No doubt! Risky? Certainly! Worth it? John says, "Absolutely!"

Other times it can't be done with that precision. Paul found a wallet at a restaurant. Careful to not look for a name in it, he took the money from it and left it where it was. Several years later this action bothered him. The real owner could have been identified at the time; now it was impossible. Paul felt better after sending a contribution to a charity.

It is possible to go too far with this and to develop an unhealthy concern about restitution. Everyone has done things about which they might feel guilty. If we chose to, most of us could spend full time trying to track down and remedy every mistake we've made. We'd never get caught up, we'd seem weird to others, and we'd neglect other important personal responsibilities.

• *Yourself*. You made the mess, so you clean it up. There is no other way.

Benefits of Apologizing

It is worth the effort to apologize. It helps the other person, but your own benefit is even greater. It frees you from guilt and shame about your behavior and, usually, from the other person's retaliation or from your fear of that retaliation.

A Vehicle for Apologizing

It is easy to learn the right words. Describe the incident you are apologizing for as simply as possible, and just say, "I'm sorry." You might say, "I spoke unkindly yesterday morning. I'm sorry," or, "When I laughed at you a little while ago, it was inconsiderate. I wish I hadn't," or, "I should have talked directly with you about it instead of talking with our neighbor. I apologize."

Two Common Wrong Turns

The most popular wrong turn is to postpone apologizing. Perhaps nothing gets more difficult at a faster rate than this. Ouch!

Another mistake is to have a "holier-than-thou" attitude about it. This is a defense against shame. We've done wrong, we know, so we want a super amount of glory for making amends. Ooops!

Shortcuts to Get There Quicker

Speak your words of apology simply and specifically. Keep it short so neither of you is unduly embarrassed. An apology need not be long nor eloquent; sincerity is all that counts.

It's easy to know how, but not easy to do. That is why we should ask God for his help. Sometimes we get annoyed with God for expecting us to apologize, and then don't ask him to help us do it. As for the pain, it will probably be greater as you seek to put your resolve into better behavior.

Examples of Easy-Way Apologies

Ineffective: I'm sorry about what I did last week; will you forgive me?

(Comment: This would be stronger if it were specific. "Owning" the problem helps build a barrier against doing the same thing in the future.)

Effective: I am sorry I made jokes about your idea in the committee meeting last week. Will you forgive me?

(Comment: This is stronger than the first example because it is more specific.)

Ineffective: I'm sure it didn't hurt you any yesterday but I wanna apologize anyhow for what I said about . . . (fade out).

(Comment: How can this person be so sure? Perhaps the apologizer would like to make a molehill out of a mountain.)

Effective: I realize now that when I called your idea stupid I was way, way out of line. I wish I hadn't. Please know that I'm sorry about it.

(Comment: This is stronger because it is based on how the offense would have affected the apologizer. Then the wounded person can say, "It wasn't such a big deal" if he or she wants to. How big a deal it was is up to the wounded party, not the offender.)

Ineffective: I guess I ought to say I'm sorry for the way I treated you.

(Comment: Does this sound sincere to you? Okay, it is hard to be sorry sometimes, isn't it? We find it much easier to think about the way we have been hurt by others than to become sensitive to the harm we do. It's

*okay to admit that it's hard, as we hear in the follow-
ing example.)*

Effective: I know my remarks at the meeting were offensive. I had some strong feelings about some things and I let
those feelings get in my way. I was wrong. It's hard to admit it,
but I was and I want you to know I realize it now. Please forgive me for my blunders.

(Comment: Let's hear four more effective apologies.)

Effective: After your husband died I started avoiding you. I
told myself you needed time alone to rebuild your life and that
I shouldn't interfere. That was a foolish lie I told myself so that I
would be more comfortable. It wasn't right. I'm sorry.

Effective: Laughing at you a while ago was inconsiderate. I
wish I hadn't. Will you forgive me?

Effective: I should have talked directly with you about
the problem instead of with our neighbor. I apologize.

Effective: I wish to ask your forgiveness for something
that came up several months ago. You asked me to help with
the potluck dinner and I said that I could not attend because I
had relatives coming from out of town that weekend. I knew
you needed help and I could have helped you, but I was too
lazy. I'm pretty ashamed about that and I'm sorry.

Apologizing Invites Confrontation

When we apologize for one of our lapses or defects, the
other person may grab the opportunity to say a few things
about our other imperfections. Wow! That doesn't seem fair,
does it? But if apologizing can be good for us, so too can
receiving confrontation.

We ought to make sure we understand the confrontation
accurately. That means listening well and then checking along

the way to make sure. You might ask the other person to re-peat to you what he has said or, even better, you can restate what you have heard so he can check it for accuracy.

Avoid the self-pity trap. If you get your car stuck in the snow, don't spin the wheels; that just makes it sink in deeper. Wallowing in self-pity is similar. Receive the confrontation and then start doing the hard work that is needed to move forward.

Try to avoid defensive reactions—arguing, not listening, or trying to explain away what the other person is saying. Avoid retaliation. When we are confronted, often the first thing we want to do is to go talk to someone else and start criticizing the person who has criticized us. Another technique more subtle and even more effective is to wait for the person who has criticized you to blunder, then make sure he or she knows that you know about it. You might even make a point of be-ing obvious about not criticizing him, or you could say to someone else, "You wouldn't believe what this person did to me." Fighting dirty, isn't it? Dastardly. But so human! Do you do it, too?

Don't brag about the amount of criticism you get. If your life is so limited that criticism is the only thing you have to revel in, you're missing out on the better parts of life.

Still, valid confrontations can be painful, and it is proper to share that pain with a trusted friend. Do that in a way that does not give an unnecessary burden to the person you are talking with. It might be best to leave out names, for example. This is especially important when the criticism was invalid or given in an unjustifiable way.

Ask yourself, *Am I doing my best with my opportunities?* In the midst of criticism that may hamper your performance in one area of life, are you still doing the best you can in the other areas?

Ask yourself, *Is the criticism valid?* If it is, it's all the more painful and you need it. Don't write it off immediately—take a close look at it. Take the words at face value. Let other people speak their minds, but for their sake and for your own do not let them be abusive.

Don't get overinvolved trying to interpret why others say what they do. Concentrate on learning what you can from the content of what they say.

Ask yourself, *Am I guilty of criticizing others?* When people criticize us, we get bent out of shape, but we go right on criticizing others. Each of us is prone to get upset about our own weaknesses when we see them in other people.

If a person confronts you with constructive purposes, it is usually an indication of deep caring for you. It is hard to remember that at the moment; in fact, the first thing that pops into your mind is probably that he or she doesn't like you. It is a beautiful thing when we have persons in our lives who love us enough to confront us about destructive or negative attitudes or behavior.

Cleaning up the messes we've made is a necessary first step in gaining release from conflict with others. When we learn from confrontations to us, and take responsibility for our offenses to others through appropriate apologies and restitution, then we can move on to forgive others.

Summary

Soon **O**ffer **R**egret and **R**estitution, **Y**ourself. Jump on it. Get it over with. Put the mess behind you and move on to better things.

Hard? Sure. But less painful than tripping over a pile of dirt under the rug. Do it.

PERSONAL ACTION PLAN

To whom do you need to apologize? No one? Hooray! Or have you been a bit hasty in your answer? Do these things:

1. At least once a day for five minutes be quiet and thoughtful, seeking to become aware of persons to whom you should apologize. Your inquiry need have but one characteristic: sincerity. Make private notes about conflicts, including minor tensions, that come to mind. These may be "tips of icebergs." *You* need to apologize! Forgive me, but I know you do. You're human.

2. When you identify an "apology project" you must carry out, commit yourself to it by signing the contract with yourself on this page, or writing one of your own.

3. Begin developing a plan for taking care of it. Use the two steps below to focus your planning.
    Write a summary of what you are apologizing for.
    Write I-statements that will help you express how you feel.

4. Fully use your spiritual resources to identify what you need to do, and then to creatively find the right method (letter, phone, or face-to-face), time and place to fulfill your apology.

Contract with Myself

Knowing how hard it is for me to apologize, I hereby agree to continue, honestly and thoughtfully, to do those things that I can do to make amends with (person's initials) _____ about the injustice I have created, and to complete all that I am capable of doing in this matter by

(date) _____.

(signed) _____ (today's date) _____

16

How to Handle Putdowns

"If brain cells were twenty-dollar bills, she couldn't buy a candy bar."

"Whatsa matter with ya? Born in a barn?"

"He so's revolting I could just barf all over him. But he wouldn't notice."

Or consider the exchange that's said to have occurred between a woman at a dinner party and Winston Churchill: "If I were your wife I would give you poison." The rejoinder, quick-witted yet equally rude: "Madam, if I were your husband, I'd drink it."

Putdowns are common. You may not know where the next one will come from.

You may be hit by the putdowns of a person who is always angry and who splatters insults like rotten tomatoes against all who come within range.

You may be an innocent bystander when a normally polite person has been aggravated to explosiveness by stressful conditions that have nothing to do with you.

Or, you may have provoked the putdown. (It will be valuable to you to analyze the times you are put down and find out if you have brought this on yourself. If you find that you have, this bad news can be beneficial to you because you can make amends for your offense against the other and then change your ways. That's a good thing because it clears up that source of aggravation in your life.)

Why Are Putdowns So Common?

While the emphasis of this chapter is on responding to putdowns, I must first vent a bit of my dismay and anger toward social factors that aid and abet this unkind behavior. I lay the largest chunk of blame upon television, especially its "comedy" programs.

The majority of relationships on dramatic or sit-com shows are unhealthy relationships. Most leading figures have serious character disorders. This has always been the meat of fiction and entertainment, but multitudes of people in our society take their lessons in human relations from TV, where moral values are upside-down. The result is an increasing number of people who are unable to distinguish fantasy from reality as they make decisions about their lives.

We were told in the seventies that the "pioneering" comedies such as "All in the Family," "Sanford and Son," and "Maude" would eliminate bigotry and other hostility by ridiculing those who embraced it. Not so. Instead, we find a new generation of shows lacking in taste and wit, and whose token gestures at redeeming value are overwhelmed by the message that vulgarity, hostility, and disrespect are funny.

That the behavior in misshapened TV families—Roseanne's, the Bundys and the Simpsons—is destructive may readily be recognized by their viewers. I hope so. It may be that no one would purposely imitate their behavior. But even if people know that the relational styles of most TV "comedies" are unhealthy, if this is all they see, where do they learn to do better?

The result is a tremendous quantity of corrosive conflict that fills the place in people's lives where caring conversation is needed. Even those who may pause to think about the pain they inflict on others with their insults justify their behavior by dismissing it as inoffensive or by drawing the target person as a vil-lain. To many, putdowns seem okay because they are so common.

Many people have lost the ability to tell the difference between insult and lively, friendly conversation. This is especially true for those people—probably a majority in our society—who believe that the world they see on television is the way the world ought to be, or the only way it can be.

The experiences many people have in their homes are even worse. An eighteen-year-old girl told me (and I have confirmation from independent sources that her report is true) that her stepfather, who has made many sexual advances to her, told her, "If you ever need spending money, just come to bed with me, and I'll make it worth your while financially." This was in the presence of his wife, the girl's mother, who, desperate for her own survival, remained silent. While this is extreme, it is far more frequent than most readers of this book would imagine.

The general insecurity of our perilous times fosters, the difficulty of attaining a sense of identity in an ever-changing mobile culture and the stress of marching at double time, as so many people must do, also contribute to the intolerance that finds expression in hostile snaps at one another.

Obstacles to Making Easy-Way Responses

I suspect, although I hope it doesn't seem like a putdown to you, that our biggest obstacle is the desire to make a sharp comeback that will bring ridicule to the other person and bring us fame for quick-witted verbal karate. But who can do that without a staff of writers? Even the brilliant literary humorist Peter DeVries, in a clever essay on the subject, declared his difficulty in finding words of rejoinder to the social jabs that came his way. He described trying to prepare his repartee in advance—a genre he called "prepartee"—and hilariously recounted his failure at luring his listeners into setting him up for the punch line.

We simply can't banter like a Neil Simon character, or snap back with punch lines crafted by a team of TV writers. But you can be the best *you* anyone can be. Instead of trying to be the best ad-lib "topper" around, why not become the ultimate *you?* It's a more worthy goal, and you can do it! You'll resist the putdown, but even better, by becoming more contented with yourself, you will be more engaging to people around you. And you will attract fewer putdowns.

Wrong Turns

For every path that takes you directly toward your goal there are many wrongs that can be made. For example, the Pennsylvania Turnpike is about as easy to follow as any road can be. Still, on a trip from Philadelphia to Pittsburgh there are many potential wrong turns. There are seventeen exits along the 270 miles between the major interchanges for the two cities. At each exit there are many options.

Even at my favorite, interchange 13 in the lightly populated mountainous region at Fort Littleton (half-way between Burnt Cabins and Knobsville), you will find six options, each a wrong turn on the trip from Philly to Pittsburgh. There must be at least 150 wrong turns that might be made on that straightforward trip.

In the area of personal relationships, which are much less tangible and in which emotions distract us, it is even easier to make a wrong turn. Here are the wrong turns most likely to be made when we have been put down:

• *We could retaliate.* If we trade insult for insult, the other person is likely to get angry and the conflict grows more vicious. Who needs that?

• *We could believe the putdown and live as though it were true.* If we believe it, we ultimately collapse under it. A young friend of mine sorted this out for himself. Here is how he described the lesson he learned: "I saw John on the street this morning. He's still mad at me. He gave me a rude gesture." Then my friend grinned and said, "No, he didn't give it to me. He stuck it out there and offered it to me, *but I didn't take it.* He's still got it. Too bad for him."

My friend had learned that he didn't have to accept trash that had been offered to him.

When you accept an insult, by believing the insult, you lose respect for yourself. If other people know that you have, even though they have not been treating you with respect, their estimation of you is diminished.

• *We could hide from the risk of being put down.* The third very popular wrong turn is simply to hide. If you are involved with people at all, you are going to be elbowed by their insensitivity from time to time. If you live like a hermit, the pain is going to fester; you will resent them and resent yourself for missing out on many good things of life.

The Map

The map for handling putdowns is divided into three parts: planning, filtering, and doing. While you will not, in the heat of the battle, have time to sit down and think things through systematically, it will be helpful to you to review some recent situations using this map. Such analysis will help you respond better on your feet when the next putdown comes.

• *Planning.* First, we shall size up the putdown. Is it important enough to talk about at all? The snide comment of a passing stranger might better be left alone. Is any harm done? The rule of thumb from professional sports—no harm, no foul— might guide you here. If it's no big deal, just ignore it.

If it's a big putdown from someone important to you, or if it's done in front of people who are important to you, that's different. Then in your best interest and in the other person's, you must stand against it. Ask yourself, *Is what was said valid?* If it's not valid, you might joke it off if you can.

For example, if a person says, "The pattern in your shirt looks like wallpaper," you might reply, "Exactly. And I'd take it off and put on a different one if it wasn't glued down!" Or you might reply,"Maybe we could arrange to have a room in your house done in this pattern." Then, if you wish, explain the facts as you see them. For example, say, "Perhaps it does, but I like the way it looks."

If the putdown targets a legitimate defect or grievance the person has against you, the style of his or her remark might be at fault while the content of the remark is legitimate and deserves your thoughtful attention. If the person has a legitimate grievance with you, the best response—best not only because it is diplomatic but best for you because you will improve yourself as a person—is to admit the deficiency, apologize, and change your ways. Easily said, no fun to do, but beneficial to everyone, especially you.

Now let's consider the needs of persons who give putdowns. Usually they do it because they are hurting. That doesn't give them a license to hurt you, but the easy-way approach takes into consideration what is in the best interest of the other persons along with proper concern for your own welfare. Try to understand them, and assess whether they are hurting. If you decide they are not, then you will deal with their inappropriateness. Hostile, abrasive behavior should be resisted. The vehicles of I-statements and confrontation are useful, as you will see in the examples later in the chapter.

If the person is hurting, the decision about what to do may be more difficult. We may help directly by some kind of assistance or at least by being a good listener. Or, we may refer the person to someone who can provide help that we cannot give. If we are in a position to help, we will use the vehicle of mirroring to understand the person's needs. In this situation it is

likely that we will absorb the putdown so we can attend to the
more worthy objective of helping him or her cope with or find
resolution of the pain.

If we decide there is no role for us to play in regard to the
pain the person is in, then we assess if it is worthwhile to deal
directly with the issue of the putdown.

It seems to me that respect for ourselves and others requires us to resist being hurt by the offenses of others except
when there is a larger good that can be obtained by absorbing
the punishment.

If you will use this step-by-step process to think through
some situations that have been part of your life, you will raise
the skills that you use when doing things on the spot.

• *Filtering.* In this situation, as in all situations described
in this book, it is worthwhile to consciously make sure you act
in ways you truly are comfortable with in the long run. Ask
yourself, *Is my plan consistent with my values?*

• *Doing.* Think about the situation as fully and as quickly
as you can, then make a plan, and check the plan against your
values. Now you know what you're going to do. So you do it.
Some familiar communication skills will help you.

Vehicles to Use As You Follow the Map

The I-statement is very handy in reporting to another person how their statement has affected you. Here are a few
examples in response to a putdown, each a little more intense
than the one before:

"I am surprised that you would say that."

"My experience with him has been quite different than yours."

"I am disappointed that you would make a remark like
that. I think you are incorrect."

"I take exception to that statement, strongly, and am offended by the way in which you said it."

"Your remark is offensive to me. Although I recognize your
right to that opinion, I find the attitude disgusting. I think it is
entirely out of place from a person in your position."

Shortcut

When we encounter any kind of difficulty, it is valuable to us to talk through the situation with a friend. Choose someone who knows you accurately but who cares enough about you to help you learn whatever would be beneficial to you to learn about yourself from this situation.

Maybe You Deserved to Be Put Down!

Suppose the putdown, although rude in style, is right on target—you *have* been _____ (whatever it is the person is accusing you of). No problem! Just look at your own behavior with as sharp an eye as you look at the other person, and if you find a mess, apologize, clean up the mess, and move ahead as a better person. What's so bad about that?

A Map for the Longer Trip Some Need to Travel

I'm sure a basketball would survive a lot better in a room full of porcupines than would a balloon, which doesn't have a tough enough skin to resist the quills it would bump into.

How thick is your skin? If the slightest touch of putdown pops your pride, maybe the root of the problem is the thickness of your self-esteem. This is such a comprehensive part of your being that it does not lend itself to quick change. There are no instant patches for punctured egos.

The long-range answer is personal growth—becoming tough enough on the outside so the quills and thorns you brush against do not let the air out of your life. It means becoming mature enough so you can react to the rudeness of others with less pain and concern about yourself, and with more caring about them, more understanding of their needs and more willingness to respond to those needs.

How do we grow basketball skin? A complete answer is beyond the scope of this book, but here are a few key elements.

1. Self-esteem comes primarily from within. Do you know what you *really* think of yourself? When people begin listening to themselves more completely, they sometimes discover that, within their own minds, they put themselves down quite often. When this pattern exists it is usually because it was learned very early in life and has become a destructive mental habit. If you do that, you need to change it, and you can change it.

2. Some self-esteem comes from outside sources: from the joy of accomplishments and recognition, for example. Develop a broad base—a variety of activities and many friends, instead of relying on one activity and one friend.

3. Bring your spiritual life into this process; you can't do without it. Thoughtful Christians know well that their worth is not earned; it is given to them undeserved by God as part of his creation design. They find immense validation of their worth in the fact that Christ came "that they may have life, and have it to the full" (John 10:10), and they experience the best of earthly joys in personal relationship with God through Christ.

4. When self-esteem is low, one's image of self tends to be defined by role, rather than as a person. For example, one might say, "I am a salesman" or "I am a cosmetologist." Roles are fine, and you ought to take delight in having a role that you enjoy. Further, as you picture yourself in your role, you ought to see success, not failure. See yourself as useful, not as a barnacle on the ship of life; see the dramatic elements of your role as well as the mundane. You ought to understand why you are in the role you are in, why you do what you do, and why you believe in and value what you do. But as you mature you increasingly see yourself as a person, not as a performer. (This is where Christianity, with the reality of relationship with God being based on grace, not works, is so life-affirming.)

5. Another strategy that helps you grow basketball skin is to give back better than you receive. Could you carry soup to a sick neighbor while you're hungry? Most of us aren't very good at that. And we're comfortable not being good at it.

For those who need to develop the basketball skin of stronger self-esteem the other strategies of this chapter will provide a measure of relief and progress while this larger, more time-consuming task is being accomplished.

Summary

The effect of a wisecrack is unpredictable. What may tickle the ribs of one person may feel like a poke in the eye to another. How we respond to putdowns is based on our values. We would all agree in principle that vicious comments (and acts) should be resisted. What is or is not vicious depends on our values.

It's not always easy to be tactful in our response to a putdown. But we can use I-statements to report how we feel. We can raise the intensity of our I-statements and use confrontation as needed so we clearly but respectfully resist the demeaning intrusion the putdown makes.

Along the way we look for our offenses against others that provoke them into the putdown. If we have been at fault, we apologize, make amends, and change our ways.

PERSONAL ACTION PLAN
Part I

This personal action plan summarizes the map given in this chapter. It will help you think through a situation so you can prepare and carry out an action plan. Use this quick process, then make your plan specific and commit to it on the next page.

Planning: I think about the putdown and plan an appropriate response.

1. Other persons' behavior. They may not have the facts, so I test what they have said against my own judgment. Do the circumstances make what they have said important? If the answer is no, go to 3.

2. Other persons' personal needs. Often, people give putdowns because they are hurting. I will try to understand them. Do I think they're hurting?

   If no, go to 6.

If yes, answer this: Is what they have said valid?

If yes, answer this: Am I likely to help that hurt (directly or by referral)?

If no, go to 4.

If no, go to 6.

If yes, go to 5.

If yes, go to 7.

Filtering: I ask myself, *Is my plan consistent with my values?*

Doing: I carry out my plan.

3. Ignore it.

4. A. Joke about it.
   B. Explain facts as I see them.

5. A. Admit and apologize.
   B. Change my ways.

6. A. Deal with the putdown.
   B. Change the subject to something that interests the others.

7. A. Use mirroring to understand their needs better.
   B. Deal with or ignore the putdown.

PERSONAL ACTION PLAN
Part II

(Situation) _____

with (person) _____

After thinking this through with the help of the easy-way map, the action plan that seems to fit best is: (list items from previous page) _

_____

_____

_____

Write out what you will say, depending upon the action you have decided on. These may be I-statements to report to the other persons how you feel about what they have said, or comments to help them understand you better, etc.

_____

_____

_____

_____

_____

_____

If you discover that indeed you have been out of line and have some fence mending to do, go to chapter 15 for an action plan.

This is my best plan.

(signed) _____

(date) _____

17

How to Ask for a Raise

Remember the first time you asked for a raise? It was probably something like, "Mommy, buy me some more candy!" Maybe you added to the emotional appeal by gazing at her with tender, pleading eyes and looking angelic and irresistible. If that failed, you may have begged and wheedled, "Everybody else gets some."

If persuasion by positive attraction didn't work, you may have resorted to ugliness: whining and the ever-popular childish tantrum. As we grow older, whining and tantrums don't work as well. We change our technique so we can better appeal to the person in control—or should I say that we give our whining and tantrums more subtle form?

Obstacles

But as the potential rewards get greater, the obstacles get larger. Some of those obstacles may be within you, but if they are, you can fix them. If you are afraid to ask, you can understand why those fears are irrational and then develop strategies to push beyond them.

If the obstacle is low work performance, asking for a raise will not be productive. Better for you to eliminate that obstacle by bringing performance up to the standards that will make you eligible for consideration. If you don't know how your performance is viewed, you can ask how you can become more valuable to the company.

If the obstacle is that you are not well known to the people above you in the organization, you probably can improve that situation through more frequent and more vivid communication. But people who are outstanding producers are known in their organizations, so if you're somewhat anonymous, find out why.

There are obstacles you cannot control. For example, you cannot control the health of the national economy, yet that influences your income potential. You can do very little by yourself to improve your company's strength within its industry. So if the nation is in recession, your industry is slumping, or your company is weak, the decision makers in your company may know that you deserve a raise and want to give you one, but these factors may prevent it.

The wage systems of highly structured organizations may limit how and when you can be rewarded. In these situations your way of getting more money is to do something different. Take that on directly by asking your immediate superior what you can do to improve your value to the company. Ask about the career paths for your kind of work. Do not be bashful about being ambitious and committed about progressing in your work. Talk about this, not as an individual who wants to getting ahead, but in terms of how you can be useful to the person you work for and, in a larger sense, the entire organization.

So, the first task in asking for a raise is to assess your own performance, your level of productivity as it is seen by the decision makers.

Wrong Turns

Probably the biggest mistake employees could make is to ask for a raise when they don't deserve one. They are asking the wrong question at that time. They should ask about how to improve, not for more money. If you prepare yourself with the suggestions in this chapter, you will avoid that wrong turn.

The first step in getting ahead is to avoid doing the things that annoy the boss. A survey of more than a hundred supervisors resulted in this list of the nine most irritating habits of workers:

1. *Procrastination.* Putting things off has a chain reaction. A missed deadline in one department usually disrupts other departments, creating friction that middle managers must resolve.

2. *Sloppy or incomplete work.* If you can't deliver the goods, the boss gets irked.

3. *Passing the buck.* Bosses can live with employees who accept responsibility for their mistakes much more easily than with those who cover up or blame others.

4. *Pretending to know what you're doing when you don't.* This kind of phony baloney drives supervisors up the wall.

5. *Lack of initiative.* Those who think like a peanut will earn peanuts.

6. *Gossiping.* Rumors and wild tales break up the harmony, lead to mistrust and unhappiness, and create the need for the leader to be a firefighter. Swapping gossip may earn you a few cheap thrills with your peers, but it won't earn you extra pay. Which would you prefer?

7. *Going over your superior's head.* This undermines their authority, threatens their sense of control and identity, and is one of the most certain ways to get on their list of people they don't want to reward.

8. *Idle chatter.* Employees who chitchat with other employees reduce the work output of two people at once. That's another sure way to miss being on the reward list.

9. *Laziness.* Working more slowly than one is capable, not paying attention to quality, being chronically late, stretching lunch or coffee breaks, and other types of indifference to output are not worthy of the basic level of pay, let alone premium pay.

What do you have *your* sights set on? Avoid these wrong turns so you can travel to the rewards you are capable of.

No matter how rich and generous a company may be, if your personal balance sheet carries more liabilities than assets, you don't deserve a raise and will probably put yourself at risk by asking. When you ask for a raise and don't deserve it, it may be a wrong turn off a cliff.

The Map

The first part of vocational success is to know what is expected on the job. You can't even know if you are matched well with a job until you know what the expectations are. So find out what the boss wants.

Preparation

Know the duties. You need—and deserve—a job description or some equivalent description of your duties. Only from such a statement can anyone determine if you are successful or not. If this is not clear, ask that it be defined. In a large organization the job description is probably in place when you arrive. In smaller organizations, or in more unique and higher level positions, the job description may be negotiated when you are hired. In such positions, duties may change substantially in a short period of time so that it would be beneficial to review that prior to negotiating about money.

In addition to needs and desires about your performance that are specifically related to your job, there are many other characteristics that are universal. These are increasingly important as the business world becomes more competitive.

Consider:

1. *Old-fashioned work ethic:* arriving early, staying late, taking work home if need be, and volunteering to help out during crunch times.

2. *Enthusiasm for the work, the company, and the people around you.* If you're not enthusiastic about your job, you may be doing the wrong thing or doing it at the wrong place. Job satisfaction is literally a matter of life or death. Studies show that job satisfaction is the best predictor of longevity. Liking your work has more influence on how long you live than genetics, diet, or even cigarette smoking. Find a job you like and cultivate it by liking the job you find.

3. *High moral/ethical standards on and off the job.*

4. *Cleanliness and systematic approaches in your work area.*

5. *Congeniality, and other old-fashioned virtues such as tact, courtesy, and respect.*

6. *Knowing when to talk.* A valuable employee is genuinely interested in other people, affirming and building up colleagues.

7. *Feeding the grapevine only those things that are true and appropriate.* Refuse to take part in office rumors.

The next station on our map is to evaluate why you deserve a raise. Asking for a raise is a selling job. So now you prepare your sales pitch. You've already evaluated whether you have a product to sell. If you don't have a good product, avoid that wrong turn. Improve your product before you try to sell it at a higher price.

Why are you worth more money? Do your homework to prepare your sales presentation. You have found out what your boss wants from you. Go through that carefully so you can, in your own notes, rate yourself on your performance, item by item, on the tasks in your job description.

How much more money do you deserve? Gather the best information you can about salaries in other companies. It would be a major tactical error to talk about other salaries within your company, except to state your expectation that you will be paid as much as other people in the company who are giving comparable performance for similar duties.

When you seek a raise, you are not asking for charity, you are selling a product—your services—to the organization. Do what effective sales persons do: Develop an appeal that makes sense to your prospect, in this case the supervisor or other decision maker.

As part of your preparation, role-play your request to your boss with a friend. This should probably not be someone from work. You are not trying to memorize an entire speech, but are firmly planting the main points in your mind and gaining confidence that you can express them readily, briefly, and forcefully. Practice will help your nonverbal communication style as well as the content.

Think all this through from the viewpoint of the person you will be talking with. In simple terms, the tug of war is this: You want more money; he or she wants more performance. So your presentation is to demonstrate that you are being highly productive. Use language that makes sense from the boss's perspective.

If you find that you don't have enough information to make a sales presentation that will speak the boss's language—that is, a presentation that will show the boss why you are contributing so much to the organization that you deserve more money—it would be better for you to get clarification about the expectations for your work. That will help you prepare for a second conversation, perhaps a week or two later, when you will ask for the raise.

Timing and Setting

Take the initiative. Don't wait for your boss to bring up the subject of a raise; do it yourself. If your performance is strong, your relationships healthy, and your presentation straightforward, it is unlikely that anything worse will happen than a rejection of your request. Indeed, you are likely to earn some respect for taking the initiative to better yourself.

Ask in advance, "Could we schedule a few minutes to talk about my performance on the job?" Your strategy is to show that you are so valuable to your immediate superior and to the company that you deserve more money. (Whether you need it or not is of no consequence to the company. Leave that out of the conversation.)

Content

State the purpose of your conversation. Describe how you perceive yourself as being valuable. Connecting this directly with your job description (or other company standard for your performance) strengthens your case. Your contribution does not have to be one big thing; the cumulative effect of many smaller contributions may be equally worthy of reward.

Describe what you want. Be specific. It is generally best to be reasonable about the amount you request, rather than overstating your request with the expectation that you will be bargained down. If you have tangible data that show how you arrived at figures—for example, salaries for comparable work in similar organizations—present that.

Communication Style

Be honest and direct without being arrogant or overbearing. You do not need to tiptoe around your request. You do not need a long build-up. Speak with confidence, minimizing the hesitations in your voice. Don't be timid. Don't fidget or toy with objects.

If you get a little flustered in the presentation, that's okay; just move ahead. If your mistake is a major fumble, correct it. Say, "That's not quite what I meant to say. Please let me rephrase that."

Steady eye contact will gather respect. It shows that you are listening carefully and shows that you expect the other person's attention, too.

The issues at stake are serious. Jokes and smiling are more likely to work against you in this situation than to be beneficial. They may even be interpreted as lack of confidence in the request that you are making. Being more serious and thoughtful in demeanor—a poker face—is appropriate to the occasion and is usually associated with maturity in your approach to work.

A short pause, about a count of three, before answering a question will not be detrimental to the flow of conversation and will indicate that you are being thoughtful, as indeed you are.

Avoid asking questions that can be answered with a quick yes or no. Can you offer two options, either of which is suitable to you? A study done in a military chow line brought striking results. The private on the line was dishing up apricots. When he asked, "You don't want any apricots, do you?" 90 percent of the soldiers declined. When he phrased, "You *do* want apricots, don't you?" 50 percent said yes. But when he asked, "Will you have one dish of apricots or two?" 50 percent of the soldiers took one dish and another 40 percent took two. That man could really sell apricots!

What you are selling is an even better product—you—and the success or failure is of great importance to you. So, be thoughtful in your preparation and presentation.

Outcome

Your request may be denied. It may even bring some feedback you don't want to hear. But you can use that to your advantage by accepting the criticism without groveling or becoming defensive, but by looking the boss in the eyes and accepting responsibility.

Never show anger when you are criticized by the boss. The boss is always right, even when wrong. Use the occasion to correct any shortcomings. In such a meeting, set time for change—perhaps a month—then discuss your progress in correcting any dissatisfactions that have been expressed. Express thanks for the conversation.

Don't go away mad. Go away with thoughtfulness and determination. Reassess the situation and begin two kinds of preparation: (1) improving yourself at your present job, and (2) looking elsewhere.

Vehicles for Conversation

I-statements will be a mainstay in your presentation. They may be about your enthusiasm for your work, boss, company, or colleagues. For example:

"I enjoy working here."

"Our company does many good things to help our community, which is one more reason I'm proud to be part of it."

"One of the best parts of my life has been the last six months since I was given more responsibility. I'm very glad to have been given the chance to tackle more difficult work, and I think I've done well."

"You have taught me a lot, not only about the job but about personal work habits, and I really appreciate that."

The I-statements may be about your performance, as you see it. For example:

"It's important to me to do well. I believe I have."

"I've spent some time the last two weekends looking at my job description and rating my own performance. I feel very good about the quality and quantity of my work."

The communication vehicle of mirroring can be useful. You may use it to mirror what you believe to be in the other person's experience, such as, "I know you have a lot of things to do, so I'll get right to the point. My purpose in this meeting is. . . ."

Or, you may respond to what the other person says, by saying: "You mentioned waiting to find out if the federal contract will be renewed. I've been aware that you have been working very hard on that. It must be difficult to put those huge proposals together and then have to wait for the response."

Confrontation is a vehicle to use only rarely in this situation. It would be more likely to be appropriate in a situation where an agreement has not been fulfilled. In this situation, you might say, "When I was hired it was with the understanding that after I had experience with each of the three product lines, I would automatically receive a 4 percent raise. This has not happened, and needs to be given attention along with the merit increase I am inquiring about."

Shortcuts

In the long run, success comes most lavishly to those who concentrate on doing well with the tasks at hand, who maintain congenial relations with all, and who line up their vocational efforts so they lead to a worthy destination. With strong performance along a track that leads to increasing responsibility, rewards will be more than adequate in an economy and context that is healthy. That's the long-range shortcut.

Dean Smith, one of the stellar college basketball coaches in history and mentor to a considerable number of outstanding coaches who have passed through his influence as players or assistants, was recently quoted as advising one of his assistants to pass up some rather attractive major university coaching jobs. "Wait for the right one," Smith reportedly said. "Vocational success begins by selecting the job where you belong." He was talking about job match—finding the job in which your special blend of talents and interests can be used and be appreciated. The relationship with satisfaction and longevity was mentioned above. If that is lacking, perhaps a lateral change would be more rewarding to you than money.

As to shortcuts for the asking process itself, there is no substitute for developing a strong, genuine enthusiasm for the persons you work with and for. The vehicle of mirroring will help you allow them to be comfortable being themselves around you, with the result that you know them more completely. If you are a person who cares about people (as I hope you are, for life is more meaningful that way) this will make it easier for you to accept their rough edges, and it will smooth *your* rough edges, so all of you are more comfortable with one another. That will raise productivity and increase the tendency of the decision makers to reward you financially. But know that if you try this without being genuine, it will fail.

Summary

Successful people want to earn money. But they earn it by concentrating on production, not on reward. Thus, the first task in asking for a raise is to learn what production the pay-givers want. Then learn how to demonstrate to them that you are worth more money. Work so that your continuing to work for them is an offer they can't refuse.

PERSONAL ACTION PLAN

(Check each when completed.)

___ Get current job description.

___ Rate my performance:

    ___ List strengths. (This information will be part of my "sales presentation" when I ask for my raise.)

    ___ List areas (as specifically as possible) to improve. (This is private, unless these topics are brought into the conversation by the boss. In that case, it will be helpful to be able to say that I have an action plan for improvement already underway.)

___ Write I-statements

    ___ about what I like about the company.

    ___ about what I like about working for the supervisor.

    ___ about my performance on the job.

___ List evidence why I am valuable

    ___ specifically to the interests of the supervisor

    ___ to the company in general

___ For each item that needs improvement, I list two ways in which I can improve. I prepare an action plan for improvement in those areas, with dates to complete the personal development, and sign it.

(signed)_____

(date)_____

18

How to Respond to a Person Who Is Angry

There are many angry people around, aren't there! We generally are rather uncomfortable being near anger, but it may be necessary for us to talk with people while they are expressing their anger. You can do so with confidence and success if you understand and use the simple guidelines in this chapter.

Two Obstacles

Angry people scare us, and rightly so, because they are unpredictable and their behavior can be dangerous. Our fear triggers biological activation in us—our bodies prepare to fight or flee. In this condition, it is hard to stick around and help an angry person settle down.

Further, we are likely to assume that the anger is directed at us, or that we are being blamed.

Sources of Anger Explosions

Quite often we are only an innocent bystander at someone's tantrum—a threatened bystander, but innocent. The outburst of angry behavior has nothing to do with us and practically no connection with what is going on at the moment.

To understand why that is so, imagine that you have a balloon that has no air in it and you are holding it by its neck, letting it dangle. If you poked that limp balloon with a pin, what would happen? Nothing much. The balloon would move aside, that's all.

Now imagine that you blow enough air into it to fill out its shape. It is round, about the size of a golf ball, with just a dab of air in it. Poke it with the pin. The pin makes a slight dimple as you push, but the balloon is soft enough to tolerate the pin. No pop.

Now imagine that you blow the balloon up tight and touch it with the pin. BANG!

What causes the noise when the balloon pops? It's not the pin, it's the pressure inside.

We have all read about people going on a murder spree and those who know the murderers saying, "I just can't believe it. He was always so pleasant," or, "She was a quiet woman who never had a harsh word for anyone." Those people were probably ones in whom pressure had been building and building until finally they had a terrible emotional explosion! It's the pressure, not the pin.

I'll explain more about the causes of anger later in the chapter. For now, since occasionally you or I may be around a person when he or she "explodes," let's consider how to respond.

Wrong Turns: How Not to Respond to an Angry Person

To begin learning how to respond to an angry person, we'll first examine four ways to do it wrong. Each of these is guaranteed to make matters worse. If you are like the rest of us you will remember having used at least one of these approaches sometime, perhaps even recently.

If you recognize yourself in any of these, give yourself a pat on the back for being courageous enough to have an open mind. It is, after all, good for us to learn from our weaknesses. That is "beneficial bad news" you can use to improve your life skills.

In this example, two neighbors are talking. One of them, a retired gentleman, spends lots of time taking care of his yard. He rushes around with scissors to clip any stray blade of grass and thinks that everyone else should have a showplace yard. As we listen in on a windy day in the fall, this man is angry. He talks to a neighbor who has not read this book, and so responds with an ineffective style. As you listen, think how you might feel if you were the angry man.

ANGRY PERSON: Just look at that! My yard is all full of leaves. And they are off your trees. See—this is a maple leaf. You have maple trees; I don't. Why can't you keep your stupid leaves raked up so they don't come over into my yard? It isn't fair!

INEFFECTIVE STYLE 1, THE DELAY: You're too upset to talk with right now. It isn't worth my time to talk with you while you're acting this way. I'll talk about it later, but I won't talk with you while you're all worked up over nothing.

ANGRY PERSON: Humpfff!

(Comment: The first ineffective style was the delay. The delay style says, in words and by nonverbal means, that you will not talk with the other person until he or she stops being angry. The angry person would already have stopped being angry if that were possible. This is a disrespectful style that says, in effect, "When you are angry, you are not good enough to take seriously." When you push persons away with the delay style it probably causes them to feel rejected, which gives them one more reason to feel angry. The most likely effect of this style is that the angry person becomes angrier.)

INEFFECTIVE STYLE 2, THE BRUSH-OFF: [After the angry person's outburst, the other person walks away without saying anything.]

ANGRY PERSON: Whoa! Wait a minute, you can't just walk away without saying anything! You come back . . . Well, of all the nerve!

(Comment: The second ineffective style was the brush-off. There was no verbal response to the angry person, but a potent, discourteous nonverbal message by ignoring the outburst and walking away. Again, it will most likely lead an angry person to become angrier. Ignoring a person is the supreme insult. This says, in effect, "You do not exist." Since anger is frequently used to get attention, ignoring angry persons further frustrates and annoys them. Sometimes, though, ignoring an outburst of anger is the right thing to do. This is most likely to be the case when the person repeatedly uses anger to try to manipulate you. In that situation, confront the person about it when he or she is not angry. Tell the person you will ignore him or her if he or she does it in the future.)

INEFFECTIVE STYLE 3, THE RATIONAL APPROACH: Oh-h-h, I don't see that there is any harm done. My leaves blow into your yard, but yours blow across the street. It ends up the same. Anyway, you pick up your leaves with your lawnmower. It isn't any harder, even if there are a few extra—which there aren't. You don't have anything to get upset about.

ANGRY PERSON: Arrrgmmmmmnh!

(Comment: The third ineffective style was the rational approach. The angry person was offered reasons why he should not be angry. There are two likely effects: The angry person does not accurately hear your explanations, so they are wasted, or the angry person hears but argues about it. A person who is full of emotion is greatly limited in the ability to listen to reason. Your explanations may seem like personal rejections. The person may be expressing anger as a way of getting understanding, not to get information, so the information is wasted. The information may be valid and may be useful later, but this is not the time for it.)

INEFFECTIVE STYLE 4, FIGHTING FIRE WITH FIRE: What's the matter with you? Are you some kind of nut? You act like you fell out of a tree! I can't make the wind stop blowing. If you don't like my leaves in your yard, you can pick them up and stick them back on the branches for all I care!

(Comment: The fourth ineffective style was to fight fire with fire. You decide you don't have to take that guff from the angry person, so you return more of the same, only louder. The effect is predictable: Conflict grows. The other person comes in on the attack and you respond with counterattack. The other person is likely to come back with more powerful weapons. What begins as a cheap shot or a shouting contest becomes a war. Who needs that?)

Generally we get back from others what we give. Give force and you'll get force in return. The best you can hope for in a contest of force against force is a short-term, hollow victory.)

You and I can do better than that if our attitudes are better: if we prefer to cooperate than to conquer. If we would rather understand other persons than dominate them. If we choose to build friendships, not to create enemies. Let's discuss how we can respond effectively to an angry person.

A Map for Responding Effectively to an Angry Person

Raise the white flag. Let's declare a truce on this melodrama and talk about what we've heard: four styles of ineffective response. The easy-way map is simple: Speak calmly, state that you will listen to whatever the angry person wants to talk about. If he or she is angry because of something inappropriate you have done, or something you were responsible for doing, but did not do, take care of it. If not, listen. The listening process will be a bit special, to accommodate the person's anger.

The Vehicle

The techniques are pretty simple, too. Using the easy way, you first get this message across by saying, "It's okay for you to express your anger. You and what you are concerned about are important to me." This can be said in a few words along with the gift of your attentiveness. Whatever your words are, be clear, brief, and sincere.

Now you listen. It does not mean agreeing. But if you're at fault, as soon as you know that you are, begin deciding the most right and proper way to make amends—apologizing and making restitution.

The nonverbal style is very important. Your voice should be soft and slow. Keep your body calm and avoid dramatic gestures. A posture that is relaxed but attentive is best. Your distance should not be as close as usual. The reason for these changes is that people look at the world differently when they are angry than when they are relaxed. When angry, the world seems very threatening to them. These adjustments make sure your style of response will not be threatening.

In summary, we show respect for the person with a few words, and do so without any threatening nonverbal signals. What happens?

The most likely result is that some of the other person's anger flows away. He or she will be able to talk more easily about what has led to the anger.

Sometimes when you show respect and caring to an angry person their first reaction is disbelief—they are just flat out dumbfounded—because it is the first time they have been treated with respect and acceptance while they were angry. Let's hear how a conversation using these guidelines might sound.

An Example That Follows the Easy Way Map

We return to our angry neighbor who's angry about the leaves.

ANGRY PERSON: Just look at that! My yard is all full of leaves. And they are off your trees. See—this is a maple leaf. You have maple trees; I don't. Why can't you keep your stupid leaves raked up so they don't come over into my yard? It isn't fair!

EASY-WAY: You know, that sounds like something important for us to talk about. Could we sit down and talk about it?

ANGRY PERSON: Uh, well, yeah, sure. I mean, maybe it's not that big a deal, but. . . .

(Comment: Did this follow our guidelines? I think so, but let's check. The tone of voice was neutral, kind of matter-of-fact. That's good; it avoids sounding like disapproval.

The responder showed that she cared enough about the other person to encourage him to talk; she showed that she believes the angry person is a person of worth and potential. It proved acceptance, without punishing the angry guy for the unpleasantness of his anger. If you can do that, you will get to know the person better and you may be able to help resolve the causes of his anger.)

Next, let's look at an exception to the rule. If the other person is angry at something you have done, or angry because you have not done something which you should have done, it's a different matter and it calls for a different response on your part. In such a case the best thing for you to do is to admit that you have been at fault. Apologize and do what you can do to undo the damage and put things back to the way they should be.

ANGRY PERSON: Your dog was in my yard this morning and dug a hole in my flower bed where I had just planted some spring bulbs.

EASY WAY (with apology):   Oh, me! I knew Vinnie had gotten out of the fence, but I didn't know he'd been in your yard. I'm sorry, and I want to do what is fair to make amends. Is there some way I can help you put things back?

ANGRY PERSON: Uh, well, yeah, sure. I mean, maybe it's not that big a deal, but. . . .

(Comment: When you have been at fault, there is nothing that will take the place of admitting it and patching things up the best way you can. You can ignore the mess you made for the moment, perhaps, but if you don't clean it up you will have bigger messes later.

But this angry person settled down pretty quickly and it doesn't happen that way every time, does it? It will turn out that way surprisingly often when you follow this method. But what if it doesn't? Let's suppose the neighbor isn't so cooperative about the dog, Vinnie, digging up the flower bulbs.)

ANGRY PERSON: Okay, so you help me plant the bulbs again. Big deal. What's to say it won't happen again? I think that dog of yours can jump over the fence.

EASY WAY: I guess that is something you are inclined to worry about.

ANGRY PERSON: Yeah! I don't know what that dog might do to my yard!

EASY WAY: You take a lot of pride in your landscaping, and rightly so—it's the showplace of the neighborhood.

ANGRY PERSON: Yeah!

EASY WAY: And Vinnie seems like a threat to the beauty of your yard.

ANGRY PERSON: In a way, yes.

EASY WAY: Neither of us wants Vinnie to bother your yard.

ANGRY PERSON: Well, I should hope not!

EASY WAY: I know how Vinnie got out this morning, and it was my fault. It is an aggravation for you, and that's why I want to do whatever is right and proper for me to do to fix the damage. And I certainly want to keep Vinnie where he belongs, which is inside the fence in our back yard.

ANGRY PERSON: Yeah.

EASY WAY: I don't know what else to say.

ANGRY PERSON: Uh, well, I guess that's fair enough. Uh, that's okay. You don't need to do anything, except keep the dog where he belongs.

EASY WAY: Yes, I agree, and we'll do our best. We really do feel privileged to have the beauty of your yard next door to us.

ANGRY PERSON: Well, thanks. Uh, I better get going. Bye.

A Shortcut

Remember the technique of mirroring? That's a handy way to keep your responses to an angry person on a healthy track. Note the use of mirroring and sincere compliments in the last demonstration above.

Sources of Anger Pressure

There are four circumstances that almost always lead to anger in a person:

1. *Threat*, which generates a first emotion of fear and a secondary emotion of anger.

2. *Loss*, which generates a first emotion of sorrow and a secondary emotion of anger.

3. *Frustration*, which generates a first emotion of helplessness and a secondary emotion of anger.

4. *Rejection*, which generates a first emotion of worthlessness and a secondary emotion of anger.

In these situations, anger will be greatest in persons who have low self-esteem, who have unrealistic expectations for how other people should treat them, who are mired in guilt, or who are aimless (lack a clear sense of direction) in their pilgrimage through life.

To help angry people, we would help them learn how to change the circumstances of life as best they can. We would want the person who faces threats to learn how to cope with those threats, to gain the skills to take care of himself or herself.

For the person who has experienced loss, we would help him or her find replacement for what has been lost. The frustrated person needs to develop skills to do the things that now bring frustration or to choose other activities that are rewarding but that bring less frustration. The person who has been rejected needs to develop new friendships that are rewarding and meaningful to take the place of the person who has rejected them.

These tasks are not easy. Obviously, when we have lost a loved one, that person will never be replaced, but the good news of the gospel is that even when trauma changes our life by taking away a person or a home or a job, life can still be good. It will be good in a new way.

Changing these internal conditions is also a long-term process. It may not be your task or opportunity to help a person with that at all. Take the first steps of understanding and accepting the *person* (though not condoning wrong behavior) and taking responsibility for your offenses against him or her. Let the rest develop as God directs.

Summary

Nearly always, the best first response to angry persons is to give them a chance to talk. Do that in your own way, leaving out all of the counter-arguments, criticism, and defensiveness that would only keep their anger alive and raise their defensiveness. Maybe your respectful approach will work. The fact is, usually it will work.

You can bring on the SWAT team later if you need to, but the best *first* approach is to seek to understand and accept the angry person as a person of worth and hear what he or she has to say. This offers the person a chance to settle down, at which point maybe he or she will be willing to listen to you.

The suggestions just given will guide you through the early moments of communication with an angry person. We have limited our discussion to the issues that give you the best chance for protection from the angry person's behavior. Suppose you want to do more than that; you would like to help that person get over the anger.

That's another topic, beyond the scope of these materials, but I will give you a quick starting point. First, recognize that anger is a secondary emotion. Before people feel angry, they have felt some other emotion. That emotion comes from the circumstances they are in, and the intensity of that emotion depends on what a person believes about those circumstances.

PERSONAL ACTION PLAN
Learning from the Past

When you deal with an angry person, which wrong turn are you most likely to make? Review the section on wrong turns if you need to refresh your memory, then circle the type of ineffective style you have used most often.

   1. Delay   2. Brush-off   3. Rational   4. Fiery

When was the last time you used this style?

   Person _____

   Approximate date _____

   Situation _____

Why might you have responded that way? (circle all that fit)
   1. Fear
   2. Dislike the person
   3. Caught up in your own concerns
   4. Didn't know a better way
   5. Other _____.

Write out what you wish you had said and done

   _____

   _____

As you look back on it now, did you say or do anything you ought apologize for now? (It might be helpful to read or review chapter 15, How to Apologize.) If so, what is your plan?
   1. Ignore it.
   2. Pretend I'll do it, but hope I forget about it.
   3. Apologize by (date)_____.

This is the best plan I know how to make.

   (signed)_____

   (date)_____

PERSONAL ACTION PLAN
Fixing a Current Problem

My intention is to respond effectively and respectfully to people who are angry, including my dealings with:
(person) _____ about (situation) _____

I will try to understand the other things that are going on in his or her life. I know that four circumstances almost always lead to anger in a person. This is my best guess of those conditions in his or her life. (1 = low, 10 = very high)

Threat	1	2	3	4	5	6	7	8	9	10
Loss	1	2	3	4	5	6	7	8	9	10
Frustration	1	2	3	4	5	6	7	8	9	10
Rejection	1	2	3	4	5	6	7	8	9	10

These situations are especially painful to persons whose personal resources are low. I rate those, for that person.
(1 = low, 10 = very high)

Self-esteem	1	2	3	4	5	6	7	8	9	10
Confidence	1	2	3	4	5	6	7	8	9	10
Sense of purpose	1	2	3	4	5	6	7	8	9	10
Peace of mind	1	2	3	4	5	6	7	8	9	10

This has required me to think about the person who displays anger. I am seeking to understand that person more completely, and to understand the origin of his or her anger. What might I be doing to contribute to that anger, if anything? I will thoughtfully and honestly consider what I might have done or might be doing that would generate anger within this person. Here are my ideas: _____
_____
_____

If I have something to apologize about (identified above), I will. These are other ways in which I might be useful to this person in the management or resolution of his or her anger: _____
_____
_____

(signed) _____ (date) _____